Clues to Rural Community Survival

by
Vicki Luther
and
Milan Wall

Heartland Center for Leadership Development

© Copyright 1987 and 1998 Heartland Center for Leadership Development

All rights reserved. Permission is granted for reproducing the list of 20 Clues to Rural Community Survival, with their exact wording, if the use is educational and non-commercial and credit is given to the Heartland Center for Leadership Development. No other reproduction or transmittal in any form is permitted without the express written permission of the Heartland Center for Leadership Development.

Heartland Center for Leadership Development
941 "O" Street, Suite 920
Lincoln, NE 68508
Phone: 402-474-7667; Fax 402-474-7672
URL: www.4w.com/heartland/

Book Design: Libby Mortensen

Printed in the United States of America

Library of Congress Catalog Card Number: 98-87755

ISBN 0-9666699-0-8

Contents

Preface 1
Background Information 3
Some Ideas on Using CLUES 7
20 Clues to Rural Community Survival .. 9
An Annotated List 11
Case Studies
   Algona, Iowa 17
   Broken Bow, Nebraska 25
   Chadron, Nebraska 31
   Cheney, Kansas 39
   Clifton, Illinois 45
   Coopersville, Michigan 53
   Eustis, Nebraska 59
   Geneva, Nebraska 67
   Hartley, Texas 75
   Jackson, Minnesota 81
   Larimore, North Dakota 89
   Lyons, Nebraska 97
   Rosholt, South Dakota 105
   St. Paris, Ohio 113
   Superior, Nebraska 121
   Watsonville, California 129
   Wausa, Nebraska 139
   Wray, Colorado 147
About the Heartland Center 155
Author Information 157

Preface

Since this study was first published in 1987, hundreds of copies have been distributed to local governments, Chambers of Commerce, economic development organizations and a wide range of community leaders in almost every U.S. state and Canadian province.

The information has been used as a discussion tool in many Heartland Center leadership programs, workshops and conferences. Local leaders have used Clues to Community Survival as a discussion topic in more than 125 town hall meetings and forums. In such discussions, participants have been asked to reflect on their own community's strengths and weaknesses as a first step towards developing a strategic outlook on the future. The Clues have been either the focus or an important part of numerous presentations and keynote speeches at conferences throughout the country. In addition, the Clues continue to attract considerable attention from the news media in this country, in Australia and in Ireland.

In every case—requests for the publication as well as with program participants—the response to the Clues has been overwhelmingly positive. The dialogues and discussions prompted by the report have also provided us with insights and information valuable to our work. This enthusiastic response has confirmed our opinion that positive information is highly motivating and that many, many small towns in our country have not only the wisdom and resources to survive but the local leadership as well.

Our thanks is extended to the many community residents who offered their time in the interviews, research and review necessary to produce these case studies. Support in the early stages of this work came from the Nebraska Policy Research Office and the Search For Solutions program of Pioneer Hi-Bred International, Inc. Staff and associates both past and present who have assisted over the years include: B.J. McGee, Ernesto Castillo, Jr., Troy Gagner, Nicki Zangari, Rod Hansen, and Marian Todd.

Vicki Luther
Milan Wall
July, 1998

Background Information

Why are some rural communities coping with fundamental restructuring when others seem to have surrendered to crisis?

With that question in mind, the Heartland Center for Leadership Development began in the mid-1980's an in-depth study of five rural Nebraska communities with populations ranging from 450 to 6000. The communities were selected from among 20 small towns that were identified as surviving the economic trends stemming from the worst agricultural economic crisis since the Great Depression. The communities were selected by the Nebraska Governor's Policy Research Office, which sponsored the study. The communities were selected based on a review of:

- census data
- labor market statistics
- geographic representation
- population size
- nominations from people knowledgeable about the state's communities

These five communities were the original case studies that eventually led to Clues to Rural Community Survival. These case studies were developed to:

1. Provide an alternative, positive perspective on rural communities that might contrast with the "dying community" image that had become commonly accepted.

2. Provide information to state legislative and executive branch leaders for potential use in guiding programs of state government.

3. Provide an information base for leadership development activities aimed at leaders in rural communities.

And it was this latter purpose that has formed the core of the Heartland Center's approach to program and materials design for leadership development.

Method of Study

The development of these case studies has followed a traditional process for the collection of both quantitative and qualitative information. As a first step, available information about each community was collected as background information. This information typically was requested and received from state and federal data banks regarding population changes and profiles, retail, labor and tax statistics, and general history of the community. Next, community leaders were identified and contacted. In each community, positional leaders were interviewed first, and then they were asked to nominate others who had influence and visibility in the community. These reputational leaders were also interviewed. In-person interviews were used and often supplemented with telephone interviews.

An interview protocol was established and staff and associates were trained in both the questioning sequence and the note-taking procedures. This was done to establish some parameters of standardizing the collected information.

The series of questions were framed around these four topics:

■ Local Economy

■ Leadership Activities and History

■ Quality of Life

■ Planning for the Future

Within each topic, the interviewers were trained to question the informant about the past, the present and what they expected to develop in the future.

All information collected in the interviews was combined with the interviewer team members' impressions, other informational materials from the community itself and data from outside sources. Once all of this information was amassed, it was used to write the community profiles found in this volume. Then, the profiles themselves in addition to all the collected information about the communities were analyzed to determine characteristics that were held in common.

Developing Conclusions

The comparison of profiles, baseline data and opinions from the interviews led to the synthesis of characteristics common to community success. These insights were reconsidered each time another community profile was added and eventually, the list was formalized into the list of Clues to Rural Community Survival found in this volume.

Other researchers have used the list of characteristics in continuing efforts to study effective community and economic development projects. Notable among these researchers were Cornelia and Jan Flora in their study of community-generated or self-development efforts and Daryl McKee in his study of economic development advantages.

It is important to remember that Clues to Rural Community Survival is descriptive, qualitative information. It does, of course, include the influences of opinions of community residents and the researchers themselves. It was never intended to serve as a quantitative or statistical study but rather as a collection of motivational profiles of communities that have had success despite all the odds. The intended audiences for this work are the community leaders and activists and the service providers assisting small towns.

Some Ideas on Using CLUES

As mentioned earlier, many communities have used the list of Clues to Rural Community Survival as the basis for a town hall meeting or some type of community forum. The list has also been widely published in newspapers, newsletters and the like, and permission to do so is willingly granted as long as the Heartland Center is credited.

One excellent design for discussion groups organized around Clues is to seat participants at tables in groups of no more than eight.

Step one:
Each table group is then assigned this task:

First as an individual, consider this list and select three items that you think our town excels at, and then three items that represent areas where our town needs work. After each person has selected her or his items, talk as a group and agree on the table groups' top three in each category.

Step Two:
Each table should report to the entire group. A master list of areas for future work can be created by a discussion leader or facilitator. While reporting, each table should be asked for one and only one item at a time, then the next table takes a turn at reporting only one item. In this way, duplication can be avoided and each table will have the chance to contribute rather than just confirming the previous report.

Step Three:
The list of items that need future work can be treated as a possible agenda for action. At this point, participants can "vote"

using self-adhesive dots or by making check marks on the items they consider most significant. This ranking process works best if participants are asked to pick their top three or five items. The votes or check marks can be tabulated and reported back to the group. Ranking in this way offers an active and visual method of participant involvement.

Step Four:

The ranked items can be used to create citizen task forces or action teams. Participants can self-select relative to the ranked items. Some variations on recruiting for these task forces or action teams might be to post a sheet of newsprint for each of the top five items and ask individuals to sign up on the sheet if they'll come to another work session on that item. Passing around a tablet or clipboard can also be effective. Sometimes having one individual who will act as a temporary chair for a group will work well, especially if the group then gathers in one section of the room to talk about next steps. Any systematic action planning process can be used to organize involvement around the ranked items.

Any of the community profiles can also be used in a group setting. First, select which profile is most likely to be interesting and realistic to the group, then assign each table group to read and discuss the town's strengths. After some discussion, each table can report on what strengths they identified in the profile. This discussion is followed by handing out the complete list of Clues and asking participants to reflect on the list in general. (The annotated list of the Clues also can be used to offer a brief presentation of the list.) This activity offers participants a chance to read and analyze a profile, suggest what they see in the community description, and then validate their own discoveries by reviewing the complete list of Clues.

Another simple design for using Clues as a discussion tool is to assign each person an interview with a community resident. The interview takes the form of a one-to-one talk about the community strengths and weaknesses with the list of Clues as a basis.

20 CLUES TO RURAL COMMUNITY SURVIVAL

1. Evidence of Community Pride
2. Emphasis on Quality in Business and Community Life
3. Willingness to Invest in the Future
4. Participatory Approach to Community Decision-Making
5. Cooperative Community Spirit
6. Realistic Appraisal of Future Opportunities
7. Awareness of Competitive Positioning
8. Knowledge of the Physical Environment
9. Active Economic Development Program
10. Deliberate Transition of Power to a Younger Generation of Leaders
11. Acceptance of Women in Leadership Roles
12. Strong Belief in and Support of Education
13. Problem-Solving Approach to Providing Health Care
14. Strong Multi-Generational Family Orientation
15. Strong Presence of Traditional Institutions that Are Integral to Community Life
16. Sound and Well-Maintained Infrastructure
17. Careful Use of Fiscal Resources
18. Sophisticated Use of Information Resources
19. Willingness to Seek Help from the Outside
20. Conviction that, in the Long Run, You Have to Do It Yourself

20 Clues to Rural Community Survival
An Annotated List

1. Evidence of Community Pride

Successful communities are often showplaces of community care and attention, with neatly trimmed yards, public gardens and well-kept public parks. But pride also shows up in other ways, especially in community festivals and events that give residents the chance to celebrate their community, its history and heritage.

2. Emphasis on Quality in Business and Community Life

People in successful communities believe that something worth doing is worth doing right. Facilities are built to last, and so are homes and other improvements. Newer brick additions to schools are common, for example, and businesses are built or expanded with attention to design and construction detail.

3. Willingness to Invest in the Future

Some of the brick and mortar investments are most apparent, but these communities also invest in their future in other ways. Residents invest time and energy in community improvement projects, and they concern themselves with how what they are doing today will impact on the lives of their children and grandchildren in the future.

4. Participatory Approach to Community Decision-Making

Authoritative models don't seem to exist in these communities, and power is deliberately shared. People still know who you need on your side to get something done, but even the most powerful of opinion leaders work through the systems—formal as well as informal—to build consensus for what they want to do.

5. Cooperative Community Spirit

Successful rural communities devote more attention to cooperative activities than to fighting over what should be done and by whom. The stress is on working together toward a common goal and the focus is on positive results. They may spend a long time making a decision, and there may be disagreements along the way, but eventually, as one small town leader put it, "stuff does get done."

6. Realistic Appraisal of Future Opportunities

Many of the communities have already learned an important strategic lesson, namely building on your assets and minimizing your weaknesses. Few small communities believe that they are likely to land a giant industry. Many of them say they wouldn't want one if it came along, fearing too much dependence on one employer would be dangerous. The successful communities know that a more realistic approach considers the community and the region as the context for future opportunities.

7. Awareness of Competitive Positioning

The thriving communities know who the competition is and so do the businesses in towns. Everyone tries to stress local loyalty as a way to help, but many businesses also keep tabs on their competitors in other towns—they don't want any of the hometown folks to have an excuse to go elsewhere. This is an area in which the recognition of community assets—people, associations and institutions—is vitally important. The comparison of one town to another is a significant means to spur improvements.

8. Knowledge of the Physical Environment

Importance of location is underscored continuously in local decision-making, as business and civic leaders picture their community in relation to others. Beyond location, however, communities must also be familiar with what they have locally. For example, the issue of preservation and protection of natural resources must be balanced with development options. Communities that manage this balance have a long-term approach to both environmental preservation and economic development.

9. Active Economic Development Program

An organized and active approach to economic development is common in successful communities. This type of approach depends on public and private sector resources working hand in hand. Private economic development corporations are common, either as a subcommittee or an outgrowth of a Chamber of Commerce or commercial club. However, it's clear that the most successful towns emphasis retaining and expanding existing businesses as well as trying to develop new businesses. This is a "gardening not hunting" model of economic development.

10. Deliberate Transition of Power to a Younger Generation of Leaders

Young leadership is more the rule than the exception in thriving rural communities. In many cases, these young people grew up in town and decided to stay or returned later to raise a family. In just as many situations, they are people who've decided to make a life in the community even though they grew up elsewhere. However, it's typical in a successful community to have a formal or informal means for established leaders to bring new recruits into public service.

11. Acceptance of Women in Leadership Roles

Women hold positions of leadership in these rural communities and those roles extend beyond the traditional strongholds of teacher, nurse or librarian. In successful communities, women take on roles as mayors, law enforcement officers, non-profit managers, business owners, etc. In many communities, this inclusion is expanded to minorities, newcomers and all types of non-traditional leaders.

12. Strong Belief in and Support of Education

Good schools are a point of pride as well as a stable employment force, and rural community leaders are very much aware of their school's importance. However, this characteristic goes beyond the K-12 system to include an approach to life-long learning that puts education at the center of many community activities. Whether adult education is targeted at skills and job performance or hobbies and recreation, the successful community makes the most of education at all levels.

13. Problem-Solving Approach to Providing Health Care

Local health care is a common concern in rural communities, but strategies for delivery vary, depending on community needs. While one community may decide that keeping a doctor in residence should be the priority, another may choose to train as many people as possible as EMTs or to use telecommunications to augment a clinic. The point here is the variety of solutions to a common problem.

14. Strong Multi-Generational Family Orientation

These are family-oriented communities, with activities often built around family needs and ties. But the definition of family is broad, and it includes younger as well as older generations and people new to the community. A typical example of this attitude is the provision of child care for community town hall meetings, thus allowing young families to attend.

15. Strong Presence of Traditional Institutions that Are Integral to Community Life

Churches are often the strongest force in this characteristic, but other types of community institutions such as newspapers and radio stations, hospitals and schools fill this role also. Service clubs retain a strong influence in social activities as well as in community improvement efforts.

16. Sound and Well-Maintained Infrastructure

Thriving rural communities understand the importance of physical infrastructures—such as streets, sidewalks, water systems, sewage treatment plants—and efforts are made to maintain and improve them. In these communities, a clean-up day includes public parks and playgrounds, business owners keep sidewalks repaired, and volunteer labor and donated materials go a long way to maintaining public buildings.

17. Careful Use of Fiscal Resources

Frugality is a way of life in successful small communities, and expenditures are made carefully. People aren't afraid to spend money, when they believe they should, and then, typically, things are built to last. But neither are they spendthrifts. Expenditures are often seen as investments in the future of the community.

18. Sophisticated Use of Information Resources

Rural community leaders are knowledgeable about their communities beyond the knowledge base available in the community. In one town, for example, retail sales histories from a state university were studied for trend information. In another, census data was used to study population change. In many communities, computer links to the world wide web have made all types of information available.

19. Willingness to Seek Help from the Outside

There's little reluctance to seek help from outside resources. These communities understand the system of accessing resources, ranging from grants for infrastructure improvement to expertise about human service programs. Competing for such resources successfully is a source of pride for local leaders.

20. Conviction that, in the Long Run, You Have to Do It Yourself

Although outside help is sought when appropriate, it is nevertheless true that thriving small towns believe that their destiny is in their own hands. They are not waiting for some outsider to save them, nor do they believe that they can sit and wait for things to get better. Making a hometown a good place to live for a long time to come is a pro-active assignment, and these local leaders know that no one will take care of a town as well as the people who live there.

Algona
Iowa

"If there weren't problems to solve, there wouldn't be a role for people like us."

—comment from an Algona entrepreneur.

Algona, Iowa, population 6,000 "and holding," is a town that's learned how to deal with crisis and keep on going—and they learned it the hard way.

Here, where an old superstition said the meandering Des Moines River would protect the town from tornadoes, a devastating twister destroyed 100 square blocks—flattening one-third of Algona's homes—on a warm summer day in 1979.

But folks who were around at the time of the big tornado say the community's response to the destruction left in the wake of the storm showed that "when the crunch comes, everybody does the right thing."

> ...*the community's response to the destruction left in the wake of the storm showed that "when the crunch comes, everybody does the right thing."*

That same pitch-in-and-do-it attitude has helped this progressive, picturesque community thrive in today's rapidly changing economic environment.

Algona has a lot going for it. Nestled in the heart of some of the richest farm land in the world, the community hosts 20 manufacturing firms, three of them on the Fortune 500 list. Two insurance companies call Algona home. There are two implement dealers, three auto dealerships, five banks, legal and accounting professionals and a full range of retail services.

Two school systems, one public and one parochial, provide K-12 education, and the Iowa Lakes Community College's Algona campus offers a four-year degree in affiliation with Briar Cliff College.

The Kossuth Regional Health Center, a totally

remodeled hospital and attached physicians' clinic, is the crown jewel in a full range of medical services available to the residents of Algona, Kossuth County and beyond. A new $2 million YMCA facility, four golf courses, six parks, eight tennis courts, two swimming pools and a lake serve the area's recreational needs.

All in all, life is good in Algona. One relative newcomer sums it up this way: "It's quiet, the people are easygoing and there are things to do here. Algona seems to perpetuate itself. The storefronts are full and the people are doing well in business. It is a growing, stable community with a diversity of ages."

> *"Algona seems to perpetuate itself. The storefronts are full and the people are doing well in business. It is a growing, stable community with a diversity of ages."*

But the things that make this town special haven't come without a great deal of hard work and dedication. Algona is a place where community pride shows and where local people work hard to keep things moving. There have been difficult times along the way, but just as was the case following the big tornado, when the "crunch" has come, everyone has been willing to do the right thing.

Most often, the right thing has been strengthening leadership, putting aside differences, and working together to plan for the future, says one Algona advocate who has been involved in a county leadership program. "We all know that the younger people can only stay here if the community thrives."

The state-of-the-art medical center is a good case in point. At one time, a few years ago, its development was in doubt—plagued by disputes over a bond issue to finance the extensive hospital remodeling. Working together, community leaders did some creative thinking about how to overcome resistance to the project and developed the community support needed to move forward. "People here are committed to working together to strengthen the community," says the executive director of the Chamber of Commerce.

Today, the Kossuth Regional Health Center challenges the definition of rural primary health care by offering advanced services, like renal dialysis, CT scanning, ACR certified mammography, ultrasound, MRI and nuclear medicine. The hospital and attached physicians' clinic share a roof with a newly constructed ambulance facility. The center is staffed with professionals with skills that could take them anywhere...but who choose to work in Algona.

> *The town benefits from "people who have a vision for the future" and a willingness to try something new– "we've had our share of failures, but also lots of successes."*

Cooperation in the community is exemplified by the two school systems. Algona's public schools have more than 1,500 students and the Bishop Garrigan schools have an enrollment of more than 800. While the two schools maintain lively sports rivalries, they more frequently work as a team to utilize local resources and to share various program offerings.

The entire community will benefit from a technology center addition underway at Algona High School. Here, area students will have access to the state's first vocationally approved video telecommunications curriculum and the opportunity to complete a four-year video telecommunications degree by taking classes offered by Iowa Lakes Community College and Briar Cliff College.

The manager of Algona's highly progressive public utility system says he thinks the town benefits from "people who have a vision for the future" and a willingness to try something new. As a community that occasionally takes a gamble, "we've had our share of failures, but also lots of successes."

Other community leaders agree.

"We have people who are willing to ask the tough questions, take the risks," said one of the town's business leaders. "People here are really devoted to making Algona better. One of our weaknesses used to be that we didn't always work together, but we've gotten better at that."

Learning how to solve problems in the past has taught Algona how to deal more effectively with such situations in the future. A local educator says community leaders have learned that "how you manage a controversial issue is as important as the subject of the controversy itself."

> *Community leaders have learned that "how you manage a controversial issue is as important as the subject of the controversy itself."*

Algona is a place that's doing a better job of getting young people into leadership, too, says a business leader who's lived here for nearly 40 years. "We're keeping the senior citizens involved, but when it's time, they're able to step into the background and gracefully let go."

One of those younger leaders, who moved here recently and served a stint as president of the Algona Chamber of Commerce, agrees. "We have a variety of newcomers with new ideas to offer, plus drive and a lot of persistence."

Clues To Rural Community Survival

One outcome of that leadership is the new YMCA facility. In 1987, after identifying a need for additional recreational opportunities in Algona, the community raised $400,000 to construct the Algona Recreation Center, a 5,000-square-foot facility featuring two racquetball courts, an exercise room and locker rooms. The concept was so popular that it soon became clear that a larger recreation center was needed.

As a result, a team of volunteers set to work to raise $1.6 million in contributions from area residents and businesses to construct a 27,000-square-foot addition. In September 1995, the new addition was dedicated and the Algona Recreation Center officially became the Algona Family YMCA. Plans for a third phase addition are already underway. More than a place for recreation, "the YMCA is a source of pride when new companies are looking at Algona," says a leader in the facility's development.

"People here have a way of getting things done," says another community leader, "but they're not always the same people. We will do whatever it takes, but what we're looking for is long-lasting relationships, not just flashes in the pan that create a hundred new jobs today and then are gone tomorrow. We want the relationships to be good for the community, good for the employer, good for the people who work there."

The general attitude in Algona is that things are going well, thanks primarily to revitalized leadership and cooperation.

> *"We will do whatever it takes, but what we're looking for is long-lasting relationships... good for the community, good for the employer, good for the people who work there."*

But there's still recognition that the community has to keep at it.

For a few years, the increased cooperation in Algona was useful to respond to situations as they arose, says one of the new class of community leaders. "We reacted to all the plant expansions and so forth. We learned to work together on that. Now we're taking the next step by proactively planning for our community's future. We're thinking and working together, trying to figure out where we want to be in five or ten years."

> *"We're thinking and working together, trying to figure out where we want to be in five or ten years."*

The answer to that challenge, like the challenges of the past, is an attitude...an attitude that says it can be done.

An area entrepreneur, whose pallet manufacturing company is one of Algona's local business success stories, says, "It takes a healthy balance of attitudes—positive attitudes that will feed on themselves and bring about positive events."

Problems aren't the main difficulty, he says. It's how local leaders respond. "If there weren't problems to solve, there wouldn't be a role for people like us."

"People don't survive in the Sandhills if they aren't self-reliant. That goes for communities as well."

—comment from a Broken Bow resident.

The town square in Broken Bow, complete with trees, park and bandstand, is a small town treasure. It offers the visitor a strong sense of the past and an immediate feeling for the community. Lined with small businesses, the square presents a picture of people shopping, walking to cafes and lunch spots and stopping to talk. But the picturesque town square also represents the challenges facing this community in the Sandhills of Nebraska. Keeping the storefronts filled and maintaining activity around the square in these times of economic change symbolize the on-going efforts to maintain Broken Bow's economic well-being.

> *"We've had periods of regression and periods of progression in our community. We keep on looking for ways to make things work."*

"Of course we lose businesses from time to time…losing the J.C. Penney store was a terrific problem. But now that space is occupied by a dance studio. The parents who bring their kids there for a dance class stop to shop and that's what we want," explained one community leader. "We've had periods of regression and periods of progression in our community," another says. "We keep on looking for ways to make things work." Today, all the buildings around the square are full. They're not all retail businesses, but there are no vacant storefronts.

Broken Bow is a community that works hard to turn problems into opportunities. With a population around 3,800, the town enjoys a location that puts it "on the way" for many travelers. Those travelers, driving both east and west, have a considerable impact on the community. Perhaps more important is the impact of the 365-employee Becton-Dickinson Vacutainer systems plant. As one business owner explained, "Because of that plant, we have a revolving group of talented, interesting people who live in our town. They bring new ideas and new energy—a great resource for us."

People seem to be one of the community's greatest resources. While Broken Bow residents will mention the excellent schools, the variety of health care facilities and social services that may make the town into a major retirement community, residents always turn back to the people of Broken Bow as the factor that will keep the community strong in the future. "People here know they can make a difference," said one business owner.

Economic development activities have given Broken Bow a fairly high profile in the state. There's been a real feeling of action in the community since the establishment of "The Nest Builders," an organization of energetic residents from Broken Bow and surrounding communities dedicated to strengthening the entire area. Realizing that Broken Bow has felt the impacts of the changes in the farm economy, Nest Builders are determined to discover ways to renew the local economy. They hold regular meetings and work as a team to develop the economy. They've helped attract new businesses to town and supported the construction of a new 60-unit retirement center. Recently, they worked with a young dental school graduate who has purchased a building and is setting up practice.

> *Residents always turn back to the people of Broken Bow as the factor that will keep the community strong in the future. "People here know they can make a difference."*

Not all of the new business comes from out of town. In recent months, some 15 local residents have set up home-based businesses in the area. "We've tried to keep our approach to economic development wide open," commented one Nest Builder. "We've encountered some resistance to change, but the action types will pull others along."

Broken Bow has enjoyed the support of local residents who chose to share the results of their successes with the community. The Melham family, for example, has made several sizable contributions to the town that required matching funds from residents. One result is a remarkable health care facility. There are many other examples of this type of loyalty on the part of Broken Bow natives. "Every town will talk about problems of consumer loyalty, but Broken Bow has been incredibly lucky to have the loyalty of locally owned firms and the Melham contributions," said a community leader. "There's no doubt their help has made this a better place to live."

> *"Certainly there are leaders that you would ask for help but, these days, that means a fairly large group of individuals who are willing to work together, not just a small group of controllers."*

Leadership in the community today is widely shared and diverse. Many residents commented that no small group controlled the town but, as one community member explained, "Certainly there are leaders that you would ask for help but, these days, that means a fairly large group of individuals who are willing to work together, not just a small group of controllers." Another said, "This is a very open town. If a newcomer arrives and wants to work for the community, it's really easy to take on a leadership role."

Getting and using help from outside resources is an approach that community leadership has maximized. Networking and resource linking to state agencies and programs are part of the economic development approach at work in the community. "You may have to be persistent and, at the same time, careful to get what you need, but technical assistance and outside funding can decide the success or failure of a new small business…After all, if you don't know where to get help, you probably won't get any!" observed a Nest Builder.

The community leader also observed that Broken Bow was in a unique position to survive these hard economic times. "Unlike many other towns in Nebraska we've never been able to rely on the Interstate to bring us business. Our community has always had to compete because of our location. Economic survival has never been handed to us as a result of traffic! We have to be innovative here," she said. And innovative they are! Using the internet to market genealogy resources at the local museum has already increased traffic at the museum. And there's talk of building on the area's basic agricultural economy by catering to tourists who want to get a close look at farming and ranching. Exotic animal operations...where visitors can view Belgian horses, buffalo, emu and ostriches...add to the tourism potential.

> *"Unlike many other towns in Nebraska, we've never been able to rely on the Interstate to bring us business. Our community has always had to compete because of our location. Economic survival has never been handed to us as a result of traffic!"*

Broken Bow is also in the forefront of efforts to work on economic development from a county-wide perspective. Perhaps because the community is located nearly in the middle of Custer County, Broken Bow has maintained a position of leadership in the effort to get communities working together.

One impact of economic turmoil is an increase in church memberships and related activities. "A crisis makes people care," observed one church member. Broken Bow has a wide representation of churches, many built during the Depression. One new church has been built in the last year.

Perhaps the strain felt in the community of Broken Bow as the result of the changes in the agricultural economy has had some positive results for the town. Only a few years ago a "Rally for Rural America,"—a public event in support of farmers—attracted few citizens. Today, there is a renewed sense of appreciation and cooperation between townspeople and rural residents.

> *"It all goes back to that Sandhill brand of self-reliance. It's never been easy to make a go of it out here," said one resident, "but why would a person want to live anywhere else?"*

The increased awareness of shared economic dependence and the need for working together are very apparent in Broken Bow. The vision of the community as a retirement center—for the region, not just the immediate community—is a vision that is shared by community members and leaders. "We've identified some of our strengths. We have the right atmosphere and lifestyle here, the medical facilities and services...and I think we have something to offer in the way of a great place to retire," observed a community leader.

"It all goes back to that Sandhill brand of self-reliance. It's never been easy to make a go of it out here," said one resident, "but why would a person want to live anywhere else?"

"People come here for something that is not someplace else."

—comment from a community leader in Chadron.

Driving into Chadron, Nebraska, from the south, it's no wonder the people here think tourism will play an even stronger role in their community's development in the future. For the last few miles, you drive through Nebraska's Pine Ridge, as plateau becomes rolling hills and, finally, pine-dotted buttes. Then the highway drops gracefully into a broad and lush valley. There, the town sits, literally surrounded by the state's natural beauty.

Chadron State Park, Nebraska's oldest state park, draws tourists to the beautiful Pine Ridge for camping, hiking, trout fishing, horseback riding, and other outdoor activities. More than 70 miles of mountain bike trails offer challenging terrain and spectacular scenic views for both beginners and experienced riders.

> *It's no wonder the people here think tourism will play an even stronger role in their community's development in the future.*

Not far away, following the White River to the west, is Fort Robinson, one of the nation's most famous "Indian Outposts." This is where Red Cloud brought his people after the great treaties were signed; where Crazy Horse, the mystic Sioux warrior, died; where a young Army doctor named Walter Reed treated "Old Jules" Sandoz.

Further north, there is Toadstool Park, Nebraska's own barren, windswept badlands. Keep going, and you will reach the Black Hills of South Dakota, with their mammoth rock portraits of American presidents and multitudes of nature's own phenomena.

"Chadron: Gateway to the Black Hills," reads some of the local promotion.

Location is important here. Chadron is a town of 5,600 (that swells by some 3,000 students when Chadron State

College is in session) in an expanded community of perhaps 9,500 when you include the State Park community, the Job Corps, the Forest Service centers and the ranches in between. You'll drive more than an hour either north or south before a larger community appears on the horizon. Driving east across northern Nebraska or west into Wyoming, you'll go even further to encounter a town of comparable size.

In addition to the tourist industry, said one community leader, "we're destined to become a trade center" because of location. The town's location and geographic isolation have already defined the community as a "center of" kind of place:

- Medical facilities here are extensive, providing health care for folks from miles around.

- A new retirement center is so popular that there are already plans in the works to double its capacity.

- Human and social services are congregated here, in agencies that specialize in family planning, nutrition for the elderly, alcohol and drug treatment and other services.

- The Pine Ridge Reservation is just 20 miles north and west, and Chadron is the biggest town in close proximity to the Native American population there.

> *In addition to the tourist industry, said one community leader, "we're destined to become a trade center" because of location. The town's location and geographic isolation have already defined the community as a "center of" kind of place.*

But location has its down side, as well. Prices for retail and consumer goods are higher, one of the few complaints volunteered by local citizens. And the community sometimes feels like a "foster child" to the rest of the state. It is, after all, more than 400 miles to the state's capital city. "It's basically a three-day trip if you want to attend a three-hour legislative hearing or meet with government officials in Lincoln," says one Chadron leader.

> *"Quality of life" is on everyone's mind here, and people know what's good about it. Clean air and clear water rank high on the list, as does the attractive countryside. But so do human traits, such as a small-town atmosphere, a strong sense of community, and family orientation."*

"Quality of life" is on everyone's mind here, and people know what's good about it. Clean air and clear water rank high on the list, as does the attractive countryside. But so do human traits, such as a small-town atmosphere, a strong sense of community, a family orientation. The word "neighborly" fits nicely.

Talk about economic development and the future usually includes a discussion of quality of life issues—especially when the focus is on what the town will or won't do to attract new business. No one here suggests chasing smokestacks as essential to economic development. "We don't want large industry," said one leader in the business community. His idea of the right kind of manufacturing is the boat business that found it necessary to expand and move into new quarters, where they employ three full-time and six part-time workers. There's been talk of promoting Chadron as a good place to retire for years, and the construction and growth of the Prairie Pines retirement center has shown the community to be an attractive spot for retirees—quiet residents with constant incomes and a preference for "high-quality but not fancy" products and services.

Chadron's business community has remained solid over the years, but not without a few jolts along the way. A main ingredient in that stability is a knack for adjusting and adapting as things change. Take the railroad, for instance. Once a major employer and an important spoke in the town's economy, the railroad went out of business a few years ago—leaving behind its new divisional headquarters building in Chadron. Today, the National Forest Service makes good use of the modern facility and, while the 400 jobs are sorely missed, life in Chadron goes on.

More recently, Chadron's extensive trade area proved so attractive that Wal-Mart constructed a 110,000-square-foot Super Center on the outskirts of town. That spurred an upsurge in retail development in the area and some saw it as the death knell for the central business district. But the downtown area—site of a million-dollar renovation project just a few years ago—simply changed its face. "It's changing from strictly a business area to more of a social area," says the local economic development coordinator. There are new restaurants and a coffee shop. A western art store, flower shop and specialty sports stores. And the theater is expanding. "It's become a living main street, a place where people go to relax as well as to shop," he says.

> "It's changing from strictly a business area to more of a social area. It's become a living main street, a place where people go to relax as well as to shop."

Unlike many communities in remote locations, Chadron has not been strongly affected by fluctuations in the agricultural economy. Partly, perhaps mostly, because the main agricultural activity here is cattle-raising, not growing crops. Ranchers here don't over-extend themselves on new equipment or high-priced land. "I told the fellas down at the coffee shop that our people didn't fly as high as they did in the irrigation community," said one financial leader. "This country is a lot rougher. They can't see what their neighbors are doing, so they just plug away and keep going," he said, only half joking.

> *"I told the fellas down at the coffee shop that our people didn't fly as high as they did in the irrigation community," said one financial leader. "This country is a lot rougher. They can't see what their neighbors are doing, so they just plug along and keep going."*

That advantage has given the community's leadership an opportunity to think more about the future than to worry about immediate survival, although several community leaders say too much of the community's planning is reactive. One unique approach to future planning a few years back was the existence of the self-proclaimed "Wild Ideas Bunch." A dozen or so community and business leaders comprised the group, meeting regularly—formally and informally—to dream and brainstorm about what their community might become. The downtown improvement project is one result. The group generated an idea for a huge, enclosed mall. When the idea hit the news, "it got a lot of people working on a more sober plan," said one former member of the Bunch.

Much of the community's planning for the future is actually done by others, pretty much outside the control of community leadership. The college, the Forest Service, the State Park, and the Job Corps are all major influences on the community. Their impact is both recognized and respected. But their critical planning decisions are made elsewhere. For example, through no special efforts by community leaders, the college is at the center of an exciting program in the field of distance learning. Designated as the pilot institution in the development of the Western Governors University, Chadron State College is playing a key role in the utilization of advanced technology to make post-secondary education resources in 14 western states available to all citizens of those states.

Community leaders welcome the outside influences on their town, yet they also recognize the importance of maintaining their unique heritage. Virtually the whole community gets involved in hosting Fur Trader Days, an annual celebration of Chadron's romantic founding.

One resident identified four key leadership groups in the community, ranging from people in official positions to quiet, unassuming leaders whose opinions are highly respected. Another said the community enjoys "situational leadership," meaning that "the same person doesn't take charge each time." Service clubs are usually active in any significant planning.

> *The community enjoys "situational leadership," meaning that "the same person doesn't take charge each time."*

When people talk about their future, what you hear is what residents of many smaller communities say: We'd like to keep it about the same, maybe a little larger, more economic diversity. When Chadron's newspaper began running full-page reminders of good things about the community to "accentuate the positive rather than threaten with the negative" a few years ago, it took nearly a full year of bi-weekly publication to complete the series.

> "When there is a need," said one community leader, "we all work together and get it done."

One person who knows Chadron well describes it as a community that "knows its assets" and knows how to "emphasize its uniqueness." Its people are conservative and independent, products of a frontier heritage, no doubt. But they also know the value of cooperation, when that's what they need to do. "When there is a need," said one community leader, "we all work together to get it done."

Cheney
Kansas

"I can see how a town can die if no one does anything."

—comment from a Cheney resident.

Economic development can come in a variety of different packages. In Cheney, a small town on the plains of Kansas, it took the form of day care.

At the time, employment in Cheney was limited. There were good-paying jobs in Wichita, but it was difficult for families with young children to cope with the 30-mile commute and work schedules because there was no licensed day care in Cheney. In order to improve their economic outlook, they had to move out of town.

> *"There were lots of negative thinkers…people who said it would never go. But you never do anything if you don't stick your neck out."*

So when the wife of a local farmer picked up some good information about day care at a rural development conference, she quickly recognized the benefits such a service could bring to her community.

With the help of a local bank loan, lots of community support and donations of equipment and playthings, she remodeled a building in the middle of town and opened My World Child Care Center. "There were lots of negative thinkers…people who said it would never go," she recalls. "But you never do anything if you don't stick your neck out."

Her dream was to fill half of the 100 state-approved slots by the end of the first year of operations, but she hadn't recognized the scope of the demand. By the time My World celebrated its first anniversary, enrollment had already reached 90. Half of the parents on My World's customer list were commuting to Wichita for work; 25% were single parents. The availability of reliable, affordable day care— open from 5:30 a.m. to late in the evening—enabled parents to seize employment opportunities in the city, bringing their paychecks back home to Cheney.

My World filled the gap for a few years before a number of smaller centers, many of them providing income for women who wanted to work in their homes, took over. But in its time, My World was just what the community needed. It enabled those who wanted to enjoy small town living to remain in Cheney—and it symbolized the determination of community leaders to revitalize their town.

Unlike many small towns in America's heartland, Cheney, population 2000, is growing. Main street bustles with activity. All the storefronts are full, a new manufacturer has reopened a plant that was closed several years ago, two businesses are undergoing major expansion and a new agribusiness firm has located in Cheney. New houses are going up and existing homes sell quickly. Some of the growth is a result of urban flight, as more people look beyond Wichita toward the less complicated life of a small town.

Cheney's Ford and Chevy dealerships, owned by four brothers, are selling cars to buyers from all the bigger towns around. Growth in recent years has been phenomenal, and they're selling four times more new cars and pickups than the automakers expect.

> *Unlike many small towns in America's heartland, Cheney is growing. Main street bustles with activity.*

A local insurance business has tripled in less than six years. And the owner of Cheney Variety is competing with Wal-Mart and the larger shopping centers in nearby Wichita with a unique combination of traditional "notions" and newer retail hits, such as name-brand athletic shoes.

> *Leadership here is good at identifying what needs to be done and then getting lots of people involved in doing it.*

Keeping local retail dollars in the community is important, and Cheney businesses emphasize convenience and service with a personal touch.

Growth in the community has presented new challenges. The 40,000-gallon water tower that was adequate for many years has been replaced with a new 400,000-gallon tower, partially funded by a Community Development Block Grant and strategically placed in a developing area so some of the water lines could be included in the project. An upgrade to the sewer system is in the works, and foresight and planning may enable it to be completed without issuing any bonds.

Completion of a new nine-hole golf course—built mostly with volunteer labor—not only provides recreation for local residents, it also brings out-of-town dollars into the economy. Nearly 75% of those using the course come from outside Cheney, about half of them from Wichita.

Providing adequate day care isn't the only way Cheney residents look after the needs of the community's children. The local school is a big source of community pride. In recent years, there have been a new addition to the elementary school, improvements in older school buildings and a completely renovated and updated running track. Most recently, residents gave 60% approval to an $8 million bond issue for the construction of a new high school complex and improvements to the grade school.

Leadership here is good at identifying what needs to be done and then getting lots of people involved in doing it.

For example, Cheney is the site of the county fair, which hadn't kept up with the times. The fair was close to going under when a group of younger leaders joined the fair board and gave themselves five years to "make it grow or let it go." After just a few years of hard work, attendance at the fair reached an all-time high.

Much of the positive activity in Cheney has its roots in lessons community leaders learned at the rural development conference several years ago. One message hit home especially hard.

"We came away from the conference really believing that 'you gotta do it yourself'" says one active resident. "After the conference, we called a city-wide meeting to identify priorities and set an agenda for the community."

That meeting, and the annual Town Hall Meetings that have followed, are the backbone of the strategic planning process in Cheney. Every citizen is urged to attend and be heard, and the broad-based participation and support generated there fosters a spirit that pervades the community all year long. "Everybody gets involved on the front end, so we don't have to fight anybody on the rear end of a project."

The success of the Cheney approach has gained notice far beyond Sedgwick County or the State of Kansas. Recently, the community was honored by the International City Managers Association as the recipient of that group's Citizen Involvement Award.

> *"We came away from the conference really believing 'you gotta do it yourself.' We know something is going to happen when we concentrate on our assets and not worry about the negatives."*

Clues To Rural Community Survival

But the real payoff has been the positive thinking and positive action that is the hallmark of Cheney today. As one city official puts it, survival for Cheney is people coming together with different views of what the future ought to be, but being willing to work together once a shared vision of the future is developed. "We want whatever happens to be our choice and not something that happens to us."

> *"We want whatever happens to be our choice and not something that happens to us."*

Clifton
Illinois

"We're taking a positive attitude...making the adjustments necessary to maintain health care in the community."

—comment from Clifton hospital administrator.

Passengers on Amtrak's "City of New Orleans" could blink and just about miss Clifton, Illinois, as the train made famous by Arlo Guthrie's folk song whistles through this farm town south of Chicago.

In big-city terms, Clifton may not be much. Its 1,350 residents live pretty quiet and, as one resident puts it, "laid back" lives. The town has no industry to speak of, and its population, like that of many other small towns in America's Heartland, is growing older. What Clifton has, however, is considerable. This small community offers a quality of life that keeps attracting new residents, many of them seeking a better place to raise their children or a quiet, affordable neighborhood outside of the city.

> *What Clifton has can't be bought—a quality of life that keeps attracting new residents...*

"We've got a lot of things going for us," says a 30-year-old Clifton native who moved back to town to take over the business his grandfather started 40 years ago.

On the list of pluses, say community leaders, are a good school system, the municipal swimming pool, a new community building, tennis courts, three restaurants and a dental clinic. A healthy business climate has resulted in the expansion of several businesses in recent years. Typical is the young owner of a heating and air-conditioning company who opened a hardware store next to his business because he recognized the community's need for such a facility.

Business development is enhanced by Clifton's location. With partial funding and legal assistance from the city, a 60-acre business tract is being developed adjacent to the interstate highway. A convenience store, gas station and several fast food restaurants will soon have travelers pulling off the highway to add to the community's economy, as well as serving local customers. "It should take off," one resident says.

But finding the small-town niche in today's world can require dramatic change in a community like Clifton. Take the Community Hospital, for example. Long a source of community pride, the hospital was founded in 1955 by a local physician who put the first hospital beds in the second floor of his own home. He continued to operate the hospital for 20 years, then gave the facility to the community. Although it was housed in an old and outdated structure, Clifton residents decided the hospital was an asset worth saving. They raised $300,000 with which they secured a loan to construct a new, modern facility. "Some of the funds came in $10,000 and $20,000 pledges from area farmers, but there were a lot in $10 donations, too," recalls a local leader who chaired the hospital board for many years.

The Clifton Community Hospital prospered—growing into a modern, 33-bed facility with eight admitting physicians and 28 consulting practitioners. Some 60 employees were needed to operate the up-to-date health care center.

Finding the small-town niche in today's world can require dramatic change in a community like Clifton.

Then, things began to change. "Much of what we provide is geriatric care," says the hospital's administrator, "and with the growth of managed health care and the tightening of Medicare benefits, it became impossible for us to compete with the larger hospitals."

But rather than simply giving up, hospital officials looked for a way to continue meeting the area's medical needs. As a result, the hospital no longer provides in-patient care, but has been transformed into an ambulatory surgery center, offering a full range of out-patient surgery services. Primary care is provided through a physician's clinic next door.

"We've taken a positive attitude to the situation and have positioned ourselves for the way health care will be delivered in the future," he says. "We've made the adjustments that were necessary in order to maintain health care in the community."

Focusing on the most timely priorities may be one key to the strengths of this area, where a county as large as Rhode Island is dotted with small towns that are learning to cooperate as they face new challenges.

"We're pulling people together," says a Clifton farmer who chairs the county board and works tirelessly to help expand the area's economy. "As we get some success, people are able to overlook (the bad feelings about) who won the ball game way back when."

That cooperative spirit shows up in a variety of ways, from the food pantry run by all the churches in the school district to the efforts of business owners to avoid duplicating what can be bought in a neighboring community.

> *Focusing on the most timely priorities may be one key to the strength of the area.*

Local leaders are working together with neighboring communities to tackle problems that affect them all. The recruitment of industry and the development of affordable housing have long been stymied by the lack of a central sewage treatment facility. Today, Clifton leaders are working with their counterparts in the area to find a way to overcome that hurdle. Clifton is often seen as a partner and leader in such projects, especially with the neighboring communities four miles on either side of town.

Cooperation is also working inside town boundaries. In Clifton, that spirit has revitalized the town's business association, which counts among its 20 members most of the town's employers.

A few years ago, the association noticed that senior citizens who came to town to get their mail had stopped their practice of wandering through the stores on main street. The problem, they realized, was that the Post Office had been moved a block away, and sidewalks from the new site toward the town's shops were substandard.

So the business owners dug into their own pockets, negotiated with local suppliers, and paid for new sidewalks themselves. Those sidewalks also make it easier for family members visiting the hospital to get to a main street cafe for lunch or to the downtown gift shop opened by one of the growing number of local business owners.

The local business association has been working to make it easier for people to shop and do business in Clifton, according to one local entrepreneur. They've put together a brochure highlighting what Clifton has to offer and erected a community information sign in the town park. There, passers-by can study a town map and review a schedule of community events.

> *Business owners dug into their pockets...and paid for new sidewalks themselves.*

That same positive attitude is evident at the old Chevy garage, where four businesses occupy space that sat empty after the dealership closed its doors. One of the occupants is Central Body Repair, which specializes in semi-truck service, attracting regular customers from a 60-mile radius that includes the Chicago suburbs to the north and Champaign to the south.

The body shop is owned by a husband and wife team, who developed the building and moved their business into town from the country. "We moved the body shop to town because we had a chance to buy this building," say the owners. "Clifton is a nice town. It's quiet and clean, and it has good access to Interstate 57."

> *"We moved the body shop to town because we had a chance to buy this building. Clifton is a nice town. It's quiet and clean, and it has good access to Interstate 57."*

"The move has been very good for us," they note, explaining that their expanded business has nine employees and the once-vacant building also is home to three new employers. "It was a wise decision."

As varied as Clifton's businesses may be, the community remains dependent on a fickle farm economy which has been on a roller-coaster ride since the early 1970s.

Yet one farmer, who also owns real estate and auctioneering businesses, still believes that Clifton offers an attractive haven for people escaping urban stress and that the community's long-term prospects are bright.

"We're holding our own," he says. "We have good medical services, an excellent school, few drug problems. Basically, we've got rural people who know how to work. But we need more industry."

Efforts to attract new industries are centered with the Iriquois County Board. Under the guidance of a group of young leaders who were encouraged to seek board positions, there has been a certain amount of success.

"I know we're still not moving fast enough," says the director of the county's industrial development association. "The little towns want to see action quicker. But we also need to get people to think about the long pull."

In Clifton, the "long pull" is maintaining a quality of life attractive enough to keep enticing new residents. One typical success story of how attractive the community is to outsiders is told by the young business owner whose hardware store put in a new line of house paint a few years ago.

"After making just two deliveries to my store, the truck driver for the paint company began looking for a home to buy here," he says. "He brought his wife to look at the community and they decided Clifton is just the kind of place they want to live."

> "... We also need to get people to think about the long pull."

"We're really fortunate to have a large group of young, committed leaders in our town."

—comment from a Coopersville official.

While many small towns in America are threatened by population decline, in Coopersville, Michigan, the town's leaders face the opposite problem. Here farming and urban expansion are "on a collision course," as one area farmer puts it, and the community's leaders are working overtime to maintain a high quality of life and still enjoy the benefits of population growth.

"We're really fortunate to have a large group of young, committed leaders in our town," says one businessman who served as Coopersville's mayor. "Our biggest challenge is moving into the future while keeping the small town qualities that have made our community attractive."

> *"Our biggest challenge is moving into the future while keeping the small town qualities that have made our community attractive."*

A community of approximately 3,400, Coopersville is an old logging town located about halfway between Grand Rapids, an expanding city of nearly one half million, and Lake Michigan, with its diverse recreation attractions.

Many of America's rural communities are struggling to hang on to the population they have, but Coopersville is growing steadily, as it has for nearly 40 years. And, while a lot of small towns are learning to deal with a rapidly aging population, the average age here is less than 40.

Location is important to Coopersville, situated in the center of Michigan's fastest growing county. But location isn't the only factor in this community's success.

"My first impression of Coopersville was so positive," says one resident, who moved here with her husband to open an insurance agency nearly 20 years ago. "The trees and the little creek at the entrance to town made a lasting impression on me."

The community has a reputation as a place where people care for one another and actively cooperate. Coopersville Cares, supported by local citizens through their churches, provides clothing, food and emergency assistance for the community's less fortunate. The Coopersville Area Foundation, funded through private donations, provides financial support for programs for the youth and senior citizens.

The school and the community have an unusually close relationship which has produced, among other benefits, a master plan for city-school district collaboration in recreational facilities and programs. A portion of the 95-acre school site has been developed as a family recreation and sports complex, linking existing parks with a trail system and increasing year-round use. Recreation facilities in the park have been upgraded to include a soccer complex and two new baseball fields. Recreation programs have been increased to fully utilize the new facilities.

An ambitious community education program makes school buildings highly accessible to the community's adults.

> *An ambitious community education program makes school buildings highly accessible to the community's adults.*

One adult education group, known as the "Old Kids," is an active seniors class that, in addition to sponsoring a choir, has written three local histories and plans periodic bus tours to historic sites. Other programs offer career improvement and enrichment courses to adults. The community education program has been so successful that the school board has found ways to keep it going, despite state cutbacks.

Clues To Rural Community Survival

Persistence is another community virtue. The local historical society submitted three grant requests before the Michigan Equity Fund agreed to support restoration of the Inter-Urban Depot, which was once served by an electric railway that ran from Grand Rapids toward Lake Michigan. Restoration of the depot has been completed and, with further grant support, the museum will soon be the home of a restored railway car that once carried passengers across the Inter-Urban line.

Coopersville's growth is both guarded and promoted by the area Chamber of Commerce. Today, with 100 active members and an energetic core of business leaders, the Chamber has helped to increase business activity downtown.

> *Coopersville's growth is both guarded and promoted by the Chamber of Commerce.*

Chamber activities have been strengthened by the activities of the Downtown Development Authority (DDA). Established in 1990 to take part in a state program aimed at improving the downtown areas in Michigan's smaller communities, the DDA was instrumental in pumping $1.5 million into Coopersville's core business district. Today, vacancies in the restored downtown storefronts are a rarity and joint efforts by the City Council, DDA and the Chamber promote a healthy business climate in all areas of the community.

Willingness to work hard is embedded in the local ethic, as employers both large and small have discovered.

Worker dependability is an acknowledged asset for large employers, such as Delphi Automotive Systems, which supplies fuel injectors for about 85% of GM's cars and for other auto manufacturers worldwide.

Numerous homegrown factories—producing every thing from custom millwork to mailboxes—have also prospered in Coopersville. Ottawa Custom Woods and Heath Manufacturing had their beginnings in local garages, but both have grown in the size and scope of their operations. Ottawa now employs 100 in the construction of display cases and other custom work that is distributed across the nation. At Heath, 60 employees build birdhouses and planters that also reach a national market.

Success of many small business ventures is attributable to the quality of the local workforce, according to one civic leader. "I really don't think they could have made a go of it if they didn't have employees who are highly dependable and productive. That can make or break an entrepreneur."

Manufacturing industries mix nicely, at least for the moment, with a healthy and diverse agricultural economy in Coopersville, a community where farming is still considered the economic underpinning.

Ottawa County produces, among other things, more apples than most other Michigan counties, and its dairy herds and milk production are a major economic strength. Corn and soybeans are still planted between healthy stands of tall hardwoods, and area farmers raise hogs and turkeys.

> *"I really don't think they could have made a go of it if they didn't have employees who are highly dependable and productive. That can make or break an entrepreneur."*

Farmers in the county are protected from creeping urban expansion by the tight reins of the township's planning and zoning board, which grants permits to build houses in the countryside only by exception...with few exceptions granted.

That's working for now. Yet a dairy farmer who is active in the community and school says he believes urban expansion and farming are on a collision course, headed for a crisis sometime in the future.

He and other area farmers who stop by a highway cafe for a cup of coffee agree that urban life and agriculture will face some tough questions ahead if Coopersville's assets continue to attract new people from the larger towns in both directions.

> *Coopersville's leaders are positive about growth, but they are not naive about the problems that accompany increasing population.*

Coopersville's leaders are positive about growth, but they are not naive about the problems that accompany increasing population. Some of the challenges of the future include concerns over water quality and quantity and the shortage of housing—problems that require strategic thinking at its best.

Coopersville is meeting those challenges through increased citizen involvement, better long-range planning, and the wisdom to build on community strengths.

"We have agriculture, manufacturing, and retail business in a pretty good combination right now," says Coopersville's mayor. If Coopersville is as successful in balancing those forces in the future as it has been in the past, it will maintain the qualities that make it attractive to both the old-timers and the new residents, as well.

Eustis
Nebraska

"If you're going to do something, you might as well do it right."

—comment from a community leader in Eustis.

Driving around in Eustis, Nebraska, which hugs a hill between Highway 23 and the creek south of town, you begin to see what "doing it right" means. Streets paved, lawns neatly trimmed, houses painted just right. Parks tucked here and there, with playground equipment or tennis courts.

The first thing you see when you drive into the community of 450 is the school. A complex of several buildings, it is the focal point of a consolidated school district that includes students from both Eustis and the neighboring village of Farnam. Elementary and high school students attend class in Eustis, where facilities include a 1,400-seat gymnasium and an Olympic-size indoor pool. The distance learning center in the high school consists of two computer labs where students acquire computer skills, enjoy interactive access to teachers and educational programs in other schools around the state. This concern for quality in education is evident in other aspects of community life, as well.

> *Further up the street—toward the water tower—sits the senior center, where more than half of the town's over-60 crowd stops each day for lunch.*

Downtown, across from the co-op elevator, a modern bank—one of the few locally owned, independent banks remaining in Nebraska—dominates the entry to the main street. Further up the street—toward the water tower—sits the senior center, where more than half of the town's over-60 crowd stops each day for lunch. A modern American Legion hall nearby is just one of the facilities available for community events. There's still the school gymnasium and the modern county fair building south of town. "Just follow the new road to the bridge and turn left." You find it across the street from the recently renovated ball fields where a state-of-the-art lighting system turns night into day on warm summer evenings.

In the heart of the community is the new wellness center where people of all ages receive top-notch medical care. It exists because a group of concerned citizens went to work, formed a nonprofit group, and put together the grants and matching funds necessary to transform a vacant downtown building into a modern medical clinic. Then they recruited three doctors, a dentist and a chiropractor from larger communities nearby who now staff the wellness center on a rotating basis.

> *"We're a lot like farmers in that, even when times get tough, we always know things will get better," says one local leader.*

This is Eustis, a farm community in a farm state. And just as the area's farmers have learned to survive and prosper through good times and bad, the people of Eustis have built their community through hard work, self-reliance and an undying sense of optimism. "We're a lot like farmers in that, even when times get tough, we always know things will get better," says one local leader.

Much of the character of the community relates directly to its strong German heritage—and that heritage is visible everywhere. There's the Wurst Haus, where they still make German sausages by hand, and der Deutsche Markt, a cozy boutique featuring imported German gifts and decorations. It shows up at the annual Wurst Tag festival (Sausage Day is how it translates) when as many as 3,000 people may turn out for the all-day celebration.

"When it's time to work, they bust their tails together. When it's time to play, they let their hair down," observed a transplanted Irishman. In fact, less than half of the residents of the community (defined here—by everyone—as the town plus the surrounding countryside) are of German heritage. But then new residents, said one relative newcomer, are considered "cousins" shortly after their arrival. The heritage is a rallying point.

There's a strong sense of community in Eustis, a family orientation, good relations between young and old. One church did a study several years ago to find out how volunteers might help the elderly who lived alone. "We found out that an amazing network already existed—without any organization—to pick up the mail, do the shopping, get them to the beauty parlor and back," said a church leader.

That sense of community spills over into the town's personality in many ways, such as how decisions are made. Ideas get bandied about for a long time—in the service clubs, the social gatherings, the school events, on the street corners. Someone or some group gets the ball rolling, others put in their two cents worth, some money gets donated. Soon, an idea becomes reality.

> *There's a strong sense of community in Eustis, a family orientation, good relations between young and old.*

The "real meetings take place outside the structured meetings," one resident observed. "These things overlap. They are all together all the time…things get discussed…a consensus is reached."

The track at the high school is an example. A group of community residents more or less decided that the old dirt track wasn't good enough, so they searched around till they found a pile of cinders at a coal-burning power plant 80 miles away. They talked the plant into giving them what they could carry away, and 90 Eustis area farmers each made one trip, hauling a truckload back to the school, where the cinders replaced dirt as a track surface. The same group raised the money for a curb around the track and the project was complete. No tax money, no public hearings, lots of community participation.

It takes a heavy dose of participation, not just one or two people doing all the pushing. "One person doesn't make or break a community," one resident noted.

> *It takes a heavy dose of participation, not just one or two people doing all the pushing. "One person doesn't make or break a community."*

Leadership is, in fact, diffused, although the Chamber of Commerce or the Village Board is usually involved in major projects. "The Chamber does the planning and the Board does the approving," was one description of how roles are played out. Some projects, such as a new sewage treatment plant and a new water system, were in planning for 10 or 20 years before they became a reality. Projects of that magnitude always require funding help from the state or federal governments, because the little towns just can't afford them by themselves, one community leader noted.

Smaller projects usually get done with a majority of community funds. A new ambulance was purchased a few years ago with donated money, and now 24 residents are certified EMTs. The Senior Center, a strong point of community pride, was built with local funds matching grant funds 2 to 1. Pledges, which were gathered in 60 days, were made for three years, but the mortgage was burned in two.

Today, as government funding dwindles, shortfalls in day-to-day operating funds are made up through quilting, noodle-making and other money-making projects.

Even though it is common for youngsters to graduate from the high school, go to college and build a life elsewhere, some stay in town or return later and, in fact, there's a healthy contingent of young people. One of the churches, for example, displayed a demographic chart showing that the largest number of parishioners fell between the ages of 20 and 35. Many of the town's business owners are under 40, some of them in their twenties.

As in other small towns in the rural areas, providing goods and services locally and creating job opportunities are of primary concern in Eustis. But community leaders here take a little different approach. They prefer growing their own rather than transplanting businesses from other towns. "In banking, we recognize that deposits made from outside our area because our interest rate is a little higher than someone else's can disappear as fast as they come," says a local leader. "Businesses are no different. Local loyalty is important in the long run."

> *... community leaders here take a little different approach. They prefer growing their own rather than transplanting businesses from other towns.*

The Pool Hall is a perfect example of growing business locally. A few years ago, a Eustis native cleaned up the old pool parlor and turned it into a place where folks could go for good food and good times. Surprisingly, Mexican food, not German cuisine, is the specialty at The Pool Hall ("with a capital P that rhymes with T that stands for Tacos") and it has become a favorite gathering spot for locals and visitors alike. Thanks to the local support and success of that venture, the owner has converted the old Eustis Hotel next door into a modern bed-and-breakfast.

Townspeople in Eustis are motivated, in part, by what they see going on in some neighboring villages. There, they say, some people have given up. They don't want that to happen in their town.

"Farming, the backbone of our economy, has its ups and downs," said one community leader, "and when the farmers hurt, we all hurt." Yet people are going to stick out the hard times, and optimism is a built-in value, in quantity. "It's more or less their make-up," one resident observed.

> *"No one ever gives up," said a business leader. "If we don't continue to try, we'll never better ourselves."*

"No one ever gives up," said a business leader. "If we don't continue to try, we'll never better ourselves."

Geneva
Nebraska

"It takes more than money and location to keep a community alive."

—comment from a community leader in Geneva.

To grocery shoppers in many parts of Nebraska, the town of Geneva is the home of "Auto-Gro" tomatoes. Bright red and juicy, they appear on produce shelves year-round. They cost more, but they taste like real tomatoes, not those plastic-like things that are shipped in from Latin America during the winter months, when America's produce growers take a back seat to those south of the border.

A greenhouse product, Geneva tomatoes are one of the examples of alternate farm produce in a state where traditional farming still dominates, but where farmers and communities are finding ways to diversify so their economic future isn't tied totally to traditional commodity production.

> *"A progressive bunch...the county's farmers are busy learning how to use computers to improve their management practices and how to exploit the commodity markets, rather than let the markets control them."*

A town of 2,300, barely 20 miles off of Interstate 80, Geneva is in the heart of Nebraska's deep-well irrigation country. The farmers of Fillmore County were among the nation's first to embrace modern irrigation practices. A progressive bunch now, as then, the county's farmers are busy learning how to use computers to improve their management practices and how to exploit the commodity markets, rather than let the markets control them.

And just as the farming community is seeking new and better methods, so are the folks that comprise Geneva and the other towns and villages in Fillmore County. They understand that they must continue to change and adapt if their communities—and the lifestyle they cherish—are to survive.

Heartland Center for Leadership Development

Occasionally, the road has been rocky. This is a town that has suffered a bank closing, like many other communities where farm loans constitute a significant part of any bank's portfolio. It's a town where two major industries started and then failed in not-too-distant memory. There have been the usual quota of store closings on the town square.

The town competes with its neighbor, York, to the north, where the population is three times as large and where Interstate traffic buzzes by in a steady stream, 24 hours a day, spawning discount shopping centers and fast-food corners.

But leaders in Geneva remain undaunted. Besides the tomatoes, perhaps the most noteworthy commodity in Geneva is the town's resiliency.

The factory in which a mobile home company once failed is again a beehive of activity. Now it houses a Canadian company that employs more than 30 in the manufacture of rectangular steel pipe, primarily for the construction industry.

> *Besides the tomatoes, perhaps the most noteworthy commodity in Geneva is the town's resiliency.*

With the Fillmore County Development Corporation as the driving force, several new businesses—ranging from a silk screen printing and embroidery operation, to a trucking firm, to a food corn processing plant—have opened their doors. A local revolving loan fund has been instrumental in the expansion or start up of an electrical shop, a jewelry store and a welding shop in recent years.

And while Geneva has to compete with its bigger neighbor on the freeway to the north—as well as the even larger cities of Grand Island, an hour west, and Lincoln, an hour east—being that close to a major transportation route is considered an asset here. Some economists have predicted that proximity to the Interstate highway may mean the difference between life and death for some Nebraska communities.

In fact, leaders in Geneva look forward to the planned construction of a four-lane highway that will put their town less than 20 minutes away from that vital thoroughfare.

> *They understand that they must continue to change and adapt if their communities—and the lifestyle they cherish—are to survive.*

"It's a blessing as well as a curse," says one local leader. "We know a lot of business leaves our town on that highway, but that easy mobility also means folks can still live here—and enjoy the quality of life a small town offers—without missing the things you find in a bigger city."

Geneva is a close-knit community that one resident describes as "just the right size. Small enough to know everyone, large enough for the basic services."

Here, though, the basic services are fairly comprehensive. For its size the town has more than its share of doctors, dentists and lawyers. The Community Arts Council is unique, sponsoring a half dozen or more touring theatrical performances each year. A community education and recreation program is paid for by the school, the community, and the hometown bank, each picking up one-third of the cost.

The word "excellent" always precedes "public schools" when townspeople tick off community strengths, which also include lots of churches and a country club.

Then there's the hospital, with its relatively new million-dollar long-term care wing, a mobile medical van that travels throughout the county, and lifeline telephone services for shut-ins. A new medical clinic at the hospital will bring two new doctors to town in the near future.

This is a community where the public sector is strong, and that adds stability to payroll, a fact which does not escape business leaders. In addition to the school and the hospital, Geneva is also home for the Youth Development Center, a state correctional facility. Fighting off two attempts by the state to close the center has reminded people that community pride, team spirit and local loyalty are important to survival.

Geneva is the county seat of Fillmore County, one of the 10 or 15 wealthiest counties in the state. It's a responsibility they don't take lightly.

Among the eight communities in the county, Geneva's 2,400 citizens make up nearly half of the combined "urban" population. But there's no "big brother" attitude here. Fillmore County has been collaborating, cooperating, and working together since long before it was the "in" thing to do.

> "Because of our size, we know we have to work together if any of us are to succeed."

"We don't have a choice," one Geneva—make that Fillmore County—leader says. "Because of our size, we know we have to work together if any of us are to succeed."

Since 1989, residents of Fillmore County have pooled their resources to support the Fillmore County Development Corporation, a non-profit corporation addressing community, economic, and industrial issues throughout the county.

A 15-member volunteer board of representatives from each community and the rural area governs operations that are underwritten by investments from county government, local municipalities, financial institutions, organizations, businesses and individuals.

> "Many people are very good at community organization," observed one community leader. "And lots of people are wearing lots of different hats."

The housing program is a good example of the county-wide approach. Faced with a need for affordable rental housing, the Development Corporation found the means for development of 15 duplex units. But they're not all in Geneva. The duplexes are scattered throughout six of the county's towns and villages.

Development of new leadership is also broad-based. Alarmed by a decline in persons filing for political offices throughout the county, the Development Corporation started the ODEGEO Project. Meeting monthly from September through May, ODEGEO (a Greek word meaning "to lead") class members learn more about their communities, their county, and their state. The results, they say, are beginning to show up in terms of qualified, interested candidates on local ballots.

Leadership is important here, and many people recognize it. "We're blessed with creative people and a good support network," one resident said. "Many people are very good at community organization, and lots of people are wearing lots of different hats."

Not that everything has gotten done without a struggle. One leader conceded that the community, and the county, struggled along without a master plan for many years (a deficiency that's now being corrected) and that there has sometimes been a lot of tug and pull as projects got moved along.

Bond issues for a new school and hospital additions failed several times, were modified as a result of informal "coffee shop" negotiation, and finally passed. A downtown improvement project had to overcome considerable opposition and the county-wide senior handi-van program had to leap hurdles, too.

But Geneva leaders wouldn't give up. Now those things are a matter of pride, even for many who once fought them, and folks in Geneva—and their neighbors all across Fillmore County—are looking for new challenges to tackle.

Hartley
Texas

"I learned that small communities don't have to die."

—comment from a Hartley resident.

Leaders in Hartley, Texas, are fighting an uphill battle to keep their town going. Agriculture is the backbone of the community, and Hartley has been whipsawed badly by the vagaries of the farm economy at least three times going back to the depression of the 1930s.

For some, it might be difficult to muster much optimism for the future of this unincorporated village of 300 in the northwest corner of the Texas panhandle, just an hour's drive from Amarillo. But not if you're a Trailblazer—a small group of Hartley folks who are working hard to create a new sense of community.

> "...we learned that, as individuals working together, we can make a difference in our community—and when you believe that, you tend to work harder."

It's worth the effort, they say, because their small community still offers a lifestyle worth fighting for.

The determination behind the Trailblazers was generated, says one of the community leaders, at a rural economic development conference a few years ago. "At the conference we learned that, as individuals working together, we can make a difference in our community—and when you believe that, you tend to work harder."

One of the first challenges to test the enthusiasm of the revitalized group of Hartley men and women was reuniting the citizens of the small town. "The community was separated into cliques," one of the leaders recalls. "We felt like we had to have a way of bringing people together again—but there was no mechanism for discussing community problems."

As a first attempt to get townspeople talking again about what they have in common, the Hartley Lions Club was reinvigorated after many years of inactivity. Lions members organized chuckwagon suppers, community gatherings held several times during the summer months, which sometimes attracted 100% of the community's residents. The cooperation required to pull the events off was as important as the social gatherings themselves, says one local leader who, along with his wife, cooked the victuals for the entire town.

"Rural America is taking a beating. But things aren't going to get any better unless we do something ourselves," he says. "With the chuckwagon suppers, we were trying to get a sense of togetherness."

> *"Rural America is taking a beating. But things aren't going to get any better unless we do something ourselves."*

An initial focus of Lions members was improvement of the aging Community Building, a World War II era barracks that was moved to Hartley from a now defunct air base nearby. A solar heating system, built by Lions members and financed through community contributions, was installed to prevent pipe freeze-up and reduce the winter heating bill.

The Lions continued to function for a few years before interest waned and the club again went on the inactive list. But that didn't stop the core group of leaders that had caught fire at the economic development conference. Determined to continue the good things that had been started, they adopted the Trailblazer name and forged ahead.

Work on the Community Building continues, but with a new twist. Now some of the labor for the project is provided by inmates at a minimum security prison located in nearby Dalhart. A new kitchen and other remodeling are aimed at making the hall suitable for wedding receptions, family reunions and social events, as well as community meetings. "We want to make it possible for people to stay here at home for their celebrations, rather than having to leave town," says one Trailblazer.

Other Trailblazer projects to foster community pride include a new Hartley community bulletin board on cable television and the establishment of the Hartley Community Foundation. The Foundation will funnel grants and contributions to betterment projects. Previously, it was almost impossible to obtain grant money due to Hartley's unincorporated status.

> *"Hartley was always a friendly place, but now people are more open to pulling together."*

The newest project in the works is the restoration of an old adobe jailhouse, built in the late 1800s and recently included in the national historical register. Research is underway so the restored jailhouse will be as authentic as possible.

Admittedly, the Trailblazers, who meet regularly to check on the progress of community projects, sometimes wonder whether they're just kidding themselves about making their town a better place. But others around town appreciate the work they do. As one local put it, "Hartley was always a friendly place, but now people are more open to pulling together."

A couple of positive developments in the business community also indicate things might be moving in the right direction.

A major expansion at Hartley Feeders meant additional job opportunities. Rather than having their workers commute from Dalhart, the company brought in 23 mobile homes to accommodate the new employees and their families.

More recently, a national firm aquired Thompson Agriplex, a home-grown ag-related business where 40 men and women are employed in the operation of a feed lot, mechanic shop, tire repair service, fertilizer distributor, trucking company and elevator. The new owners talk of expanding the operation and adding jobs to take care of the new business they plan to develop.

But the best measure of Hartley's potential for the future might rest with the school. The community's strong school system has always been an important community asset, and residents here have worked hard to maintain its excellence. Hartley patrons pay the highest school taxes the state allows. The investment pays off: 65% to 70% of high school graduates go to colleges or trade schools. The school consistently finishes near the top in statewide test scores.

Concerns of a just a few years ago that small schools, like Hartley's, would disappear have been eased by new regulations designed to better equalize state aid to education. The new formula benefits small schools where children are succeeding.

And the small school atmosphere at Hartley has even attracted new students. Kindergarten through 12th grade enrollment has increased by almost 50% (from approximately 125 to nearly 180) over the past decade. Parents transferring their children to Hartley from the Dalhart schools say they're seeking a return to the basics and an escape from "bigger school problems."

> *The community's strong school system has always been an important community asset, and residents here have worked hard to maintain its excellence.*

A few positive indicators, such as the increased enrollment, encourage the Trailblazers to keep on going—and remind them of what they learned in the economic development program. "If the conference did one thing for Hartley," says one Trailblazer, "it was to build some confidence that local leaders can make a difference. I learned that communities don't have to die."

Positive changes are being felt throughout the community. One area resident, who grew up in Hartley and has farmed here all his life, says he sees a lot of signs that local people want their community to survive, even against some pretty steep odds. "Tough times cause people to pull together," he says.

> *"We've got to stimulate the community, get everyone by the hand. Team spirit can get it done."*

Another local farmer agrees, "We've got to stimulate the community, get everyone by the hand. Team spirit can get it done."

Jackson
Minnesota

"You can't solve it all alone, but together we can, not just today, but everyday."

— comment from a community leader in Jackson.

When the Unisys Corporation announced on a cold December day that it was closing its computer plant in Jackson, Minnesota, the announcement sent a shock wave through the community. "There was lots of doom and gloom," says one local businessman, who owns a publishing company in Jackson and heads the industrial development group here.

> *When the Unisys Corporation announced on a cold December day that it was closing its computer plant in Jackson, Minnesota, the announcement sent a shock wave through the community.*

Yet a year later, on the first anniversary of the plant closing announcement, this town of 3,600 held a celebration. In just 12 months, it had recovered from the blow that followed the loss of 300 good-paying jobs, and it had helped to replace those jobs—and more—through new industries, plant expansions, and new business start-ups.

With the Unisys plant, which at its height employed 800, this southwestern Minnesota community had become complacent, say local leaders as they look back on those times.

"Things were rolling pretty good," says the president of the Jackson Chamber of Commerce. "We probably got lulled to sleep a little bit."

When the plant closing was announced, he says, the complacency disappeared overnight, replaced by a new leadership aggressiveness that has revitalized the town's image of itself.

"We were laying on the mat," says one community leader, a veterinarian who moved to Jackson in the early 70s. "We had to decide either to get up and fight or get counted out."

"Everyone was groping when Unisys made its announcement," admits the manager of the rural electric cooperative. But then the industrial development board got going, and things began to get back on track.

> *"We were laying on the mat. We had to decide either to get up and fight or get counted out."*

First the development board asked Unisys to change its mind. When that didn't work, the board tried to find another manufacturer to buy the building and save the jobs. Finally, the development board members decided they would have to create a solution themselves, and they spent "countless hours" doing the legwork and research to overcome the crisis.

"At the time a lot of us were overburdened," says a leader of the industrial development group who had moved to Jackson when he saw an opportunity in the printing business. He admits spending a lot of time on the project, as well as hundreds of dollars out of his pocket on telephone bills, and that his business suffered as a result.

The celebration a year later showed what a community can do if it works hard and gets all the help it can.

What Jackson did, mainly, was refuse to quit.

When it became clear that Unisys wasn't going to reopen the plant, and when no other buyer appeared immediately on the horizon, Jackson's business and industry leaders started negotiating to buy the building, situated in an industrial park created 20 years earlier to attract the plant in the first place.

The building and all its equipment, worth an estimated $1.5 million, eventually was sold to the community for less than $200,000. And somehow the development board had convinced Unisys to come up with a cash grant that the town used as a down payment to buy the building and grounds.

When the industrial board heard that a manufacturer of fiber glass truck and utility bodies was looking for a place to expand, board members went to work. Using the availability of the now-vacant building as the prime attraction, they put together a financing package with state help and negotiated job training assistance for the plant's work force. Their efforts paid off, and that company began operations, filling the void that had been left when Unisys departed.

Their new-found aggressiveness also attracted another manufacturing plant to the industrial park. With assistance from both the city and the state, Ag-Chem constructed a mammoth $8 million, five-acre building right across the road from the Unisys building. There Ag-Chem manufactures and assembles enormous big-wheel tractors that are used for fertilizer and chemical application throughout North America and the world.

And that was just the beginning. After two years, the truck body manufacturer closed down. But now, Jackson wasn't stuck with an empty building as Ag-Chem jumped at the opportunity to expand its operation. They purchased the building and spent $4 million to renovate it into a technology and education center. Today, Ag-Chem brings customers and clients from all around the world to Jackson to help them learn more about how to use its equipment and computer software in high-tech programs of site-specific application of agricultural fertilizers and chemicals.

> *Much of this growth, say company leaders, is directly related to the community's attitude.*

Ag-Chem has added some 500 new jobs to the Jackson payroll in the last five years.

Much of this growth, say company leaders, is directly related to the community's attitude.

"This community wants us to be here and we like it here," says the Ag-Chem plant manager. "When the word gets out that there's thought of expansion, they come out of the woodwork" to find out what needs doing. The company had an offer from another state, which would have given them a plant to move into. But in Jackson, "we had the total support of every government agency involved, also the townspeople in general. When all that got on the table, the decision was made. This was the place we wanted to be."

The manager of Pioneer Hi-Bred International's soybean production plant in Jackson confirms that the development board no longer waits to see what local employers' plans are. After being surprised by the Unisys decision, development board members now visit local businesses on a regular basis, asking what plans they have, and what the town can do if changes are on the drawing board.

> *After being surprised by the Unisys decision, development board members now visit local businesses on a regular basis, asking what plans they have, and what the town can do if changes are on the drawing board.*

When the Pioneer Hi-Bred plant manager told them that his company planned to double the size of its Jackson warehouse a few years ago, "the development people were out in a flash, offering help." Pioneer wasn't asking for financial assistance for its expansion, he notes, but he still felt good about the attitude. That expansion was accomplished and company officials are now contemplating a third expansion project in Jackson.

The industrial board is tuned into "jobs, jobs, jobs," says the board's president, and it doesn't let roadblocks stand it the way. Prospective employers are "courted," he says. "If they even breathe it, we try to provide it." Meetings to brainstorm possible solutions are common.

Not everything works.

"We've had some successes, we've had some failures," says one leader who's been involved in the industrial development effort for many years. Most importantly, he says, "we've had some extremely good teamwork come out of our crisis."

That teamwork isn't limited to attracting manufacturing employment. Attention is being paid to locally owned businesses, especially retail. More retail shopping options downtown would be good for the economy, attracting more dollars from the visitors who are drawn to auto races at the county speedway during the summer and keeping more college business in town year-round.

But local retailers must find a way to keep up with today's changing consumer interests and Wal-Mart-style competition. The owner of the Coast-to-Coast store expanded his business into the old City Hall with encouragement from the City Council. He is busy redefining small town retail with a one-of-a-kind hardware store. His operation now includes renting videos, handling UPS shipments, selling boats and motors, and carrying sports clothing. Retailers recognize that their best way to compete is to provide local convenience for the general merchandise that people need every day. With that philosophy, Jackson has maintained a good mix of retail stores and nearly all of the downtown buildings are full.

> *There's a unique attitude in Jackson...and that attitude says, "We'll do it!"*

There's a unique attitude in Jackson, he says, and that attitude is, "We'll do it!"

Community leadership, which underwent a transition to a younger generation, is gaining confidence. Now, say leaders young and old, the community can put up with the naysayers and withstand community controversy.

The Unisys plant closing and the crisis that followed changed the way community leaders behave. The industrial board now meets weekly to talk about what's on the agenda for the future and to evaluate how they're doing today.

Community volunteers wore themselves thin replacing the jobs that were lost when the plant closed. But they soon realized they couldn't continue at that pace on their own, so they convinced the city to hire a full-time professional. Since then, Jackson has employed an economic development coordinator who serves as the staff member for both city initiatives and the industrial group.

> *"The crisis led to better cooperation," says one local banker. As a result, "success has snowballed and generated new enthusiasm."*

"The crisis led to better cooperation," says one local banker. As a result, "success has snowballed and generated new enthusiasm."

The town continues to take advantage of whatever help is available, maintaining contact with area legislators, state agencies and foundations, and participating in rural leadership programs whenever they are available. The town's leadership has replaced complacency with aggressiveness and a new willingness to take risks.

Teamwork and leadership lessons learned through economic necessity also show up in other aspects of the community, says the town's industrial development coordinator. "I've lived and worked in other towns, and I've never seen a place where they are so good at applying leadership techniques to build community consensus," he says. He cites a recent school consolidation issue as an example. In Jackson, the issue was thoroughly thought through and discussed publicly before the community voted overwhelmingly in favor of consolidating their school with that of a neighboring town. There, the issue divided the community, leaving scars that will take time to heal.

> *The most important lesson from the plant closing crisis may be that community leaders need to keep talking, working together, taking a team approach to problem-solving.*

The most important lesson from the plant closing crisis may be that community leaders need to keep talking, working together, taking a team approach to problem-solving. According to Jackson's economic development coordinator, "You can't solve it all alone."

"But," he adds, "together we can, not just today, but everyday."

Larimore
North Dakota

"It's the people that make things happen. You get shot down, but you don't give up."

—comment from a business leader in Larimore.

Like many other small towns that dot America's rural landscape, Larimore, North Dakota, is in a state of transition. Once a bustling rail hub and commercial center, Larimore, population 1,500, has become a bedroom community. A substantial number of Larimore's citizens drive to work each day at the nearby Air Force Base or into Grand Forks, 30 miles away.

A farm community nestled into the rich Red River Valley, Larimore is struggling to redefine itself and its future, and it is still a bit uncertain about what that future will be.

> *"Sometimes we feel sort of like a boat without a rudder. Once in a while we get blown off course a bit, but we keep working to make sure we're heading in the right direction."*

"Sometimes we feel sort of like a boat without a rudder," says one local businessman. "Once in a while we get blown off course a bit, but we keep working to make sure we're heading in the right direction."

The Larimore Economic Development Corporation president, a local grocer who adopted Larimore as his home in the early '80s, is just one of a group of community leaders who are hard at work, trying to put spark into community life and pushing the town to take a new look at itself. Much of the group's involvement began a few years ago when several of them attended a regional economic development conference at which they had the opportunity to compare their community with other small towns.

Mainly, one of the attendees recalls, the conference helped him set his sights higher. "I felt like we had never dreamed big enough," he admits. "Many communities started with a lot less than we have."

Transplanting their enthusiasm back home proved to be no easy task, however. There were those who were happy with the town just the way it was. Others wanted change, but they weren't ready to pitch in to make it happen. Some even resented the efforts of the emerging community leaders. Criticism that they were "trying to take over" was not uncommon.

> *"I felt like we had never dreamed big enough," he admits. "Many communities started with a lot less than we have."*

Undaunted, the young community leaders set out to broaden the role of the town's Commercial Club. It was renamed the Community and Commercial Club—ComCom for short—in order to include men and women not directly involved in business and to welcome those living in rural areas around Larimore. Early meetings were sparsely attended, but soon there were 20 to 30 at the typical meeting. Later, ComCom would evolve into the Larimore Chamber of Commerce.

One of the more active Chamber of Commerce committees was the economic development task force. So it's not surprising that when the Chamber slowly faltered, the Larimore Economic Development Corporation was formed to assume the leadership role.

Meeting regularly for nearly a decade now, one EDC leader admits that they dream of striking it rich—attracting a big, clean industry to provide hundreds of new jobs. The same one every town would like to have. But being realistic, they recognize that their real hope lies in working hard to improve all aspects of their community, doing what they can to bring about success in manageable doses, and celebrating when those small steps are accomplished.

There's been plenty to celebrate in Larimore in recent years:

■ The modern nursing home that has been a point of community pride for several years just completed a $2.25 million remodeling.

■ A $1.9 million addition to the high school strengthened education programs.

■ New housing is being developed adjacent to the town's popular nine-hole golf course.

■ The satellite medical clinic in town added staff and lengthened its hours.

■ A local potato grower expanded his operation, adding three new warehouses and additional employment opportunities.

■ Even though the local bank was merged with a larger out-of-town institution, its commitment to Larimore was solidified through a major remodeling.

■ The owner of the car wash built a new facility, expanding to include a new laundromat.

■ When it appeared that the hardware store might close, new ownership was found to revitalize the business.

And the list goes on.

L ooking ahead, the City Council and nursing home board are studying

> *When it appeared that the hardware store might close, new ownership was found to revitalize the business.*

the feasibility of adding assisted-living apartments for the town's elderly. And the EDC—using funds generated by a new city sales tax earmarked half for economic development and half for infrastructure improvement—has acquired and renovated a 9,000-square-foot building in which emerging businesses can locate. "When we used to go recruit businesses to locate here, they always asked if there was space available," one local leader recalls. "Now that we have the space ready to go, they come looking for us."

Currently the building houses several small cottage industries, but if things work out as planned, it could soon be the home of a family-owned sewing business with 35 to 40 employees.

Looking back, one EDC board member traces the cooperative spirit that marks Larimore's development efforts to a project that came up short of success. When there was talk of building an ethanol plant in the area, Larimore put together a proposal to locate the facility in their town. They emerged as one of three finalist communities before plans for the plant were derailed and the project was canceled. But the town came out a winner anyway. "We all worked together on that proposal, and it got everyone, including the City Council, thinking about developing our community. That effort opened up lines of communication and cooperation that are still serving us well today."

> *"We all worked together on that proposal, and it got everyone, including the City Council, thinking about developing our community. That effort opened up lines of communication and cooperation that are still serving us well today."*

Another cooperative project could bring a multi-million dollar investment and nearly 100 new jobs to Larimore. The EDC took the lead in preliminary studies to determine the feasibility of making particle board from wheat straw. Funded through private donations, early studies have shown that the process works, that there is sufficient wheat straw available in the area to provide the raw material for such a plant, and that there is a market awaiting the finished product. With the support of the City Council and EDC, the corporate board of directors established to spearhead the project is developing final business plans and seeking venture capital and other funding to proceed with construction of the plant.

But developing new and expanding business and industry isn't all that's going on in Larimore. People are making other things happen, as well.

One energetic group is the Larimore Community Entertainers, a club that produces choral concerts and Broadway-style shows in a main street theater that was recently added to the National Register of Historical Buildings. Renovation of the grand old playhouse was originally undertaken by two brothers who retired in Larimore after successful off-Broadway careers. Upon their death, they donated the theater to the Entertainers group and established a trust to further the arts and entertainment in the community. Funds from the trust are used for capital improvements,

> *One energetic group is the Larimore Community Entertainers, a club that produces choral concerts and Broadway-style shows in a main street theater that was recently added to the National Register of Historical Buildings.*

while ticket sales and fund-raisers provide operating expenses for the theater.

But in spite of a generally positive attitude and notable successes in efforts to revitalize their community, leaders in Larimore still feel the ever-present threat of apathy among many citizens and are aware that they must continue to fight negative thinking.

The town needs to keep working at "making people proud of what they have" says one local business owner who grew up in the area and then decided to come back. "I could have lived anywhere," she says. "There's no place I'd rather be."

The EDC chairman admits he gets frustrated when some people just want to take care of their own business and aren't willing to work for their community. He also gets impatient when things seem to move too slowly.

But he maintains his enthusiasm about what might be: "Slowly, the people with common sense and guts will win out. They'll change things, and we'll all have a better community for it."

> "Slowly, the people with common sense and guts will win out. They'll change things, and we'll all have a better community for it."

Lyons
Nebraska

"It's hard to get the small town out of you."

— comment from a Lyons business leader.

When a local seed corn dealer invited some townspeople to "tag along" to a company-sponsored economic development conference, community building became a priority in Lyons, Nebraska. The group came away from the conference so fired up that their challenge was "how to get started in the community without blowing everybody away," recalls one of the conference attendees.

> *We were so fired up that our challenge was "how to get started in the community without blowing everybody away."*

Right away they talked to the Lyons Community Club and started a Strategy Committee for the Club. With an open membership including farmers as well as business people, the Lyons Community Club offered a perfect grassroots sounding board for new ideas.

"Grassroots" has a special meaning in Lyons. Located on the meandering Logan Creek in northeast Nebraska, some land around Lyons has several feet of topsoil—rich land for bluegrass sod. In the late '60s, an enterprising entrepreneur began cutting sod from pastures to sell in the city. Today, there are several sod farms around Lyons with hundreds of acres from which bluegrass sod is harvested. This is the largest concentration of sod farming from Sioux Falls to Kansas City and Denver to Des Moines. Mowing and cutting sod is a good source of work for young people in the summer, and one local company specializes in laying sod for developers.

Lyons celebrates its fame as the Sod Capital of Nebraska on the Fourth of July each summer with, what else, a Bluegrass Festival. The event draws some 2,500 people.

It's not that Lyons wasn't already a fine community before the conference created an upsurge in interest in the community development process. Folks have always been proud to call Lyons home—and with good reason.

As in other healthy rural communities, Lyons supports an excellent school system. Bond issues consistently carry on the first vote. The area enjoys good medical services, including a regional hospital in a neighboring town just a few miles away, a physician's clinic in Lyons and a reliable volunteer rescue squad. Cooperation among the churches in Lyons is counted as a big plus for the town, and the elderly population is also considered a strength. A manor on the edge of town and apartments for seniors attract elderly retirees.

Businesses in town include a bank, a hardware store, a furniture store and a prosperous grocery that is large for a town of just 1,100 people.

The town has some homegrown industry. Swine Service Specialists telemarkets a special hog feeder internationally from an office on main street. The feeders are made by a local custom manufacturing company, Brehmer Manufacturing. An industrial development group attracted Brehmer to Lyons several years ago with a large vacant building as the major enticement. "The building looked pretty empty when we first moved in," recalls the owner of the manufacturing company. "We just steadily filled it up." Both businesses have seen steady growth and expansion in recent years.

> *Lyons is a town that draws people home. Retirees, farmers and professional people have moved back for the quality of life.*

Lyons is a town that draws people home. Retirees, farmers and professional people have moved back for the quality of life. "Towns all have a distinct personality, and Lyons has always been a sedate community—comfortable,

Clues To Rural Community Survival   99

friendly and a nice place to live," says a local attorney who has served as a Community Club officer.

There was a feeling that life was good in Lyons before leaders attended the economic development conference some time ago, but there was also a concern that the community was becoming a bit stagnant. When the group returned from the conference, that suddenly changed. The new Community Club Strategy Committee began to meet regularly at 6:30 in the morning. The public was always invited and all meetings were reported in the local paper.

The Strategy Committee had learned that "homespun ideas are the ones that catch fire." So they invited broad-based participation with surveys and town hall meetings. Over 30 ideas for community projects were proposed, and soon several of these projects were underway, involving as many volunteers as possible.

It was decided to promote Lyons as the Sod Capital of Nebraska. A special logo was developed and a postmark touting the Bluegrass Festival was arranged to go on every piece of mail that leaves Lyons from May 15 through July 15. Several citizens found pictures of sod houses in old family albums and in just five months, in time for the July Bluegrass Festival, volunteers designed and constructed a sod house in the city park.

> *In just five months, volunteers designed and constructed a sod house in the city park.*

A mini-park on main street was targeted for improvement. In just nine months, volunteers raised funds to install benches, fencing and a sprinkler system. The park was landscaped with shade trees, new sod and shrubs. The local VFW erected a veterans memorial in the mini-park.

One of the ideas that emerged from the town meetings was for a craft and antique co-op store. Those interested in the idea arranged for space in a downtown location and worked out contract details. With volunteer labor, they renovated the building to create 16 spaces for artists and craftspeople. Three months later, Talents and Treasures Mini Mall was open for business, drawing shoppers from all around the area. Each seller rented space for a monthly fee plus a 10% commission on items sold. The mall was staffed by the renters, each working two or three days a month in the store. After several years of successful operation, the craft and antique mall is now closed—but in its time, it provided the outlet that enabled several home-based businesses to gain a foothold in the marketplace.

The hard work and early successes of the Strategy Committee set a high level of expectations in Lyons, according to one community leader. "Even in our first years of work, we let people in the community and in other towns, as well, know that we are serious about making Lyons even better." Some projects like the sod house were chosen to show immediate results. Others took longer and showed that people can stick with it.

> *"Even in our first years of work, we let people in the community and in other towns, as well, know that we are serious about making Lyons even better."*

Perhaps the most notable of the long-term projects is the improvement of the city park. "Not long ago, people would talk about how the lagoon in the park used to be full of water for fishing and recreation," recalls a community leader. "That was changed to talk of how the lagoon could be restored."

The community rallied around the park project and $90,000 was raised from personal donations and a few small grants. Today, the lagoon has been cleaned up and stocked with fish and the area around it has been relandscaped and is being developed as an arboretum, with responsibilities for upkeep shared by the elementary school and the city's tree board. Once again, the people of Lyons can point to their city park with pride.

Funding for other future projects has been addressed even before they are identified. The newly established Lyons Community Foundation includes $80,000 in endowments, designated for community improvement efforts and a scholarship fund.

> *Not long ago, people would talk about how the lagoon in the park used to be full of water for fishing and recreation. That was changed to talk of how the lagoon could be restored.*

But, as is the case with most community development programs that rely heavily on volunteers, it has been difficult to maintain the momentum in Lyons. The group that originally caught the fever at the economic development conference has dwindled. Some have moved away; others have simply worn out. Some folks in town say things have moved too quickly, and there is the usual disagreement as to what areas of community improvement should get top priority. The Strategy Committee no longer meets regularly, although attendees at a recent town hall meeting—the first in two years—indicated that people are still willing to go to work for their town.

"After the initial rush of excitement and flurry of activity, we've hit a bit of a slump," says one of the original Strategy Committee leaders, "but that doesn't diminish what has been accomplished. We recognize that sometimes things have to take a dive before they rise up again, and we know that we've put down a strong foundation on which to build in the future. Now the community is in the process of deciding how the building blocks will be placed on that foundation."

> *"We know we've put down a strong foundation upon which to build in the future."*

Rosholt
South Dakota

"Rosholt, Proud and Alive."

—as seen on a town sign in Rosholt.

When the implement dealership in Rosholt, South Dakota, went under, it looked like area farmers were going to have to do without. For two years they'd sought a buyer. One deal looked like it was going to work out, but the financing fell through.

"The bankruptcy judge was going to lock it up," recalls one area farmer. Then he and seven other Rosholt farmers started an investment club, and the group began negotiations with the bankruptcy judge and all the attorneys. By the time negotiations were over, the farmers had formed a corporation, bought the building and leased it to a new dealer. An economic victory for the community, the deal saved five jobs and kept the parts store open for local business.

Some of the investors had to borrow the money, but that didn't hinder their determination to keep the dealership open. The risk was worth it, they say. Not only does having a local dealer save a 60-mile round-trip to get parts, it also speaks volumes about the lengths to which the people of Rosholt are willing to go to build a strong community for themselves and their families. Still open and going strong, the locally owned implement dealership stands as a testimonial to community pride and perseverance.

> *"Sometimes we don't appreciate what we've got until it's gone, and then it's too late to get it back."*

In rural areas, says one member of the investment group, "Sometimes we don't appreciate what we've got until it's gone, and then it's too late to get it back."

In Rosholt, population 400, it's typical behavior for the community to get behind whatever needs to get done, and then see that it happens.

The town's 75th Anniversary Jubilee is another in a long list of examples. According to the head of the community committee that planned the celebration, the Jubilee turned into a giant event that produced a profit of nearly $40,000. About half of that was earmarked for economic development.

"When anything needs to get done, it gets done," says the event organizer, whose grandfather was a community founder. "I recall once when someone's house caught fire at 6 o'clock in the morning and destroyed the roof. Everyone turned out to help and by 6 o'clock that same evening, the new roof was on."

Then there's the story of the depot. Now home to the historical society's Rosholt Museum, the neat, trim structure sits in the new park along the highway through town. But it wasn't always so.

> *The town's 75th Anniversary Jubilee turned into a giant event that produced a profit of nearly $40,000. About half of that was earmarked for economic development.*

When the 75th Jubilee Committee heard that the railroad was going to burn down the old depot—a sagging relic of the town's past—they were determined to transform the eyesore into a monument. The railroad was willing to sell it for a dollar, but only on the condition that it be moved to a new location. In a typical Rosholt teamwork effort, townspeople gingerly jacked it up and moved it across town to the highway.

"People were skeptical but not unsupportive," about the idea of saving the building, the head of the committee recalls. Townsfolk ended up donating the money to move and rebuild it, then volunteered to landscape the site. It took just ten weeks from notice that the depot was facing a bulldozer to its relocation in the new historical park. Now it serves as home to a growing collection of antiques and local artifacts.

"Nothing ever flops in Rosholt," she adds, coining a phrase that could be something of a town motto. Could be, that is, except that the town sign already carries the message: "Rosholt, Proud and Alive."

> *"When somebody comes up with a new idea, it gets talked about for a while and then, if enough people get behind it, a committee is formed and the idea gets translated into action."*

When the people of this northeastern South Dakota community want to get something done, they seem to come alive with an infectious community enthusiasm that reaches into every corner of the town and the surrounding countryside.

One Rosholt banker—who got to know the community as a newcomer several years ago—still marvels at the way people go to work for their town. He says when somebody comes up with a new idea, it gets talked about for a while. Then, if enough people get behind it, a committee is formed and the idea gets translated into action. Citizens turn out in good numbers for annual town hall meetings where progress on community goals is reviewed and new objectives are discussed, listed and prioritized.

At one such meeting, a group decided the town needed street signs—not just so people would know their own addresses, but also to facilitate the growing popularity of direct parcel delivery. A committee worked on the idea, the town council approved it, and the signs were ordered. The day they were to go up, the committee worried that there wouldn't be enough help to get the job done. But this is Rosholt. One after another, townsfolk dropped other things to pitch in. "Pretty soon, we had twice as many people as we needed," the banker recalls.

A local pork producer, who is also head of the Rosholt Historical Society, notes that the community is blessed with "lots of community spirit" and what he calls "tireless workers." Among them is a group of retired farmers who live in town and donate countless hours to community projects. "I don't know what we'd do without them," he admits.

"People here work very hard for their community and they enjoy a lot of good fellowship in the process," he says. "What's that phrase, 'Tough times don't last, tough people do'?"

> *"People here work very hard for their community and they enjoy a lot of good fellowship in the process."*

Like other farm communities, Rosholt has had its tough times. Located in one of South Dakota's wealthiest farming areas, agriculture—with its economic ups and downs—is the community's backbone. But, for a town its size, Rosholt also has a healthy variety of businesses. Among them are a furniture store that sells to a market of up to 100 miles away, an auto dealer that competes in an even larger market and an elevator that has enjoyed healthy profits over the years. The Rosholt Review, a weekly newspaper with a circulation of 1,400, hasn't missed an edition in some 80 years.

"Our main street is only two blocks long, but it includes four brand new buildings," boasts one community leader. The recent arrivals include both a new community hall and a fire station. A nursing home/assisted living complex recently opened in town, a new apartment building is in the planning stage and the town recently acquired 23 acres to be developed as a new housing subdivision.

An economic development project that should bring significant growth to Rosholt will capitalize on the area's agricultural economy. A $10 million facility to convert grain into ethanol is in the final planning stage. When operational, the ethanol plant will provide 24 new jobs and add value to crops produced on area farms.

> *But the town is not without its problems. School enrollment, bolstered by transfers from a nearby town, fights to hold its own.*

But the town is not without its problems. School enrollment, bolstered by transfers from a nearby town, fights to hold its own. Potential school consolidation is a major topic of conversation in the local cafe. And with jobs in the area hard to find, most young people leave after school and don't come back.

"I'd like the school to be bigger so we could get more advanced classes," says one high school senior who, with a classmate, won a national Future Homemakers of America award and a trip to California. "We're limited as to job prospects," agrees the classmate. But they both agree that their trip to the West Coast gave them more reasons to like a small town.

Others who have left Rosholt in the past agree. "Ever since we started on the ethanol plant project, we've been getting inquiries from people who want to work there, many of them from people who moved away and want to come back home," says one community leader.

That's good news for the community that should be a boost to future economic development efforts. One attempt to improve job opportunities by recruiting a small manufacturer a few years ago had local officials wondering if an adequate labor supply existed in the area. Today, there's a sense that years of working to improve their community have made Rosholt attractive to businesses and workers, alike.

There's a healthy attitude about the future of Rosholt, says the administrator of the community-owned nursing home. One of the home's problems in the past has been a lack of qualified employees in the immediate area, with some workers commuting up to 50 miles one way each day. The labor shortage has caused problems, she says, but she's maintained a positive attitude and solutions have been found.

> *There's a healthy attitude about the future of Rosholt, says the administrator of a community-owned nursing home. "If you take the attitude that a community is going to dwindle, it will."*

The main thing that gives her confidence, she says, is the attitude of the people of Rosholt.

"If you take the attitude that a community is going to dwindle, it will. But that certainly is not the case in this town."

St. Paris
Ohio

"The community that resists change dies."

—comment from a community leader in St. Paris.

On the surface, St. Paris, Ohio (population 1,850), looks like hundreds of other small midwestern farm towns...quiet and pleasant...a nice town to drive through on an autumn Sunday afternoon.

But underneath that traditional exterior, a thriving entrepreneurial spirit breeds new businesses with an aggressiveness that can be felt from the coffee shop just off main street to the farms outside of town.

Like most small towns in west central Ohio, St. Paris enjoys a diverse economic base that would be the envy of many rural communities in other areas.

> *Underneath that traditional exterior, a thriving entrepreneurial spirit breeds new businesses with an aggressiveness that can be felt from the coffee shop just off main street to the farms outside of town.*

A huge Navistar plant, about 20 miles away, employs thousands within its giant factory compound. Just outside of St. Paris, a parts supplier for a nearby Honda auto plant employs nearly 1,000 work-ethic-happy farm kids. Like most manufacturing plants, employment levels have been up and down over the years, but the general trend has been one of steady plant expansion and growing job opportunities for local residents.

Still, the striking feature is the explosion in—and success of—new business ventures that spring up like newly planted corn, nurtured along carefully by local residents who have learned how to make St. Paris a hotspot of entrepreneurial success.

Take the story of Infotel, for example. Founded in the early 1980s, the company started out as a part-time business venture based in the home of its young owner. Raised on a farm close by, this area entrepreneur started a riding stable in college, then went on to become a veterinarian. But he never really practiced animal medicine, acting instead on business instincts that would be the envy of any MBA graduate.

The original idea was to be a distributor of computer printers in the rapidly growing personal computer market, and business was good. So good, in fact, that the operation quickly expanded into a warehouse on Highway 36, just west of St. Paris.

In less than a decade, the electronics business had grown from a home-based business with one small computer into a beehive of telemarketing and nationwide computer distribution, most of it handled by UPS semi-trailer trucks that backed up to Infotel's warehouse each morning and each afternoon, first unloading new inventory and then returning to haul away the day's sales. Soon the young company was moving 10,000 computer printers a month, gaining an impressive market share of all U.S. sales. The company was growing at a rate of 250% per year.

The company was growing at a rate of 250% per year.

But the folks at Infotel weren't satisfied. In filling their role as a distributor, they recognized a growing demand for custom configured personal computers. No other company was filling the void, so they stepped up to the plate. The distribution business continued to grow under the Infotel name, but now the plant was also the home of Midwest Micro, a builder of specially ordered, custom configured PCs.

The success story being written in this small Ohio community wasn't going unnoticed. Infotel's market niche, and its $275 million in annual sales, began catching the attention of some of the big players in the electronics industry.

In the Fall of 1997, when the company was acquired by Global Direct Mail Corp., the business that had first taken root in the mind of a young St. Paris entrepreneur became part of an electronics giant. Listed on the New York Stock Exchange, combined annual sales for the conglomerate are $1.5 billion.

But back in St. Paris, things really haven't changed all that much. Some 400 men and women from surrounding farms and communities still earn a good living at the plant just outside of town.

> "Our biggest help has been just being in a rural environment. The work ethic...that's an important part of it. It's a big strength in rural America."

The success of Infotel didn't come without plenty of hard work, recalls the company's founder, his quiet manner cloaking a supercharged ambition that has been the driving force behind the firm's mind-boggling record of marketing success. "We concentrated on doing two or three things really well," he says, pointing to price, quick shipment, and expert sales support as keys to the firm's growth.

"The big void in rural America," continues Infotel's founder "is marketing." "What's my definition of business?" he asks himself aloud. "A marketing war and an efficiency contest," he answers.

Although the auto parts manufacturer nearby has asked for and received community concessions, first for locating there and later for expanding, Infotel's founder never viewed tax incentives as a main ingredient for success. "Our biggest help has been just being in a rural environment. The work ethic...that's an important part of it. It's a big strength in rural America."

While not quite so dramatic as Infotel—yet—there are other business success stories in St. Paris, as well.

Wooden Wonders was started just a few years ago in the basement of a downtown storefront, with the owner and one or two extra employees during busy times hand-producing decorative wood plaques. Quickly outgrowing that facility, the company now occupies a 6,000-square-foot plant in a nearby community.

Marketed primarily through trade shows, nine Wooden Wonder employees are kept busy year round making plaques that have found their way to Australia, England, France, Mexico and Japan—as well as homes and offices all across the U.S.

These are just a couple of examples of the entrepreneurial spirit that thrives in St. Paris. Many of the young business leaders who call St. Paris home own one, two, perhaps three businesses that they are managing successfully. Some of them still farm a few acres, reluctant to give up their attachment to the soil that their parents and grandparents worked before them.

Product and market specialization, with an emphasis on sales via mail order to similar markets nationwide, is a recurring theme among St. Paris area entrepreneurs.

> *Product and market specialization, with an emphasis on sales via mail order to similar markets nationwide, is a recurring theme among St. Paris area entrepreneurs.*

Not all businesses in St. Paris have been developed by longtime residents of the community, however. One relative newcomer, who moved to St. Paris specifically to start his business, says he bought land here because "it was less expensive." He now grows what his neighbors fondly call "Gourmet Hay," a high-quality alfalfa that he ships by the semi load to horse lovers nationwide.

What's the difference about his hay vs. someone else's, he explains, is that "I market it uniquely," through ads in nationwide horse owners' magazines. Building on what he's learned in the hay business, he's opened a tack shop in another small town nearby, selling Australian riding equipment to passers-by and, of course, by mail order…nationwide.

Another resident of St. Paris with multiple business interests is a local seed corn dealer. A farmer at heart, this business leader has expanded his horizons during a stint as director of agriculture and engineering at the local community college. He and his wife also established a successful country dancing center and he has dabbled over the years in the auto sales field.

Most people in the community are proud of the town's ability to encourage new business development, but some are concerned, too, about the broader community impact when young people are that busy making a living.

"Thirty years ago, aggressive young people were investing in building a community. Today, we're more into investing in ourselves," said one resident. "It's kinda scary."

"They don't have time to sit down," says one long time resident, "let alone time to work on community boards, church boards, and the like."

Others agree. "Thirty years ago, aggressive young people where investing in building a community. Today, we're more into investing in ourselves," said one local resident. "It's kinda scary."

A big help in keeping the town on its feet, though, according to a St. Paris business leader, has been the Honda parts supplier, an independent company known as KTH. However, he says, he does worry about overdependence on one big employer. "We're dependent on Honda's profitability," he admits. "Very dependent. Too dependent."

The town may be doing well, he continues, in part because the farm crisis of a few years ago "made farmers into better managers, bankers into better loan officers." Now, he adds, St. Paris should think about developing the kind of strategic plan that a business would, projecting several years into the future, answering such questions as "where do we want to be in 10, 20, 50 years."

A rural chaplain for the Ohio Council of Churches, who has seen many communities work through changes, says he senses a willingness in St. Paris and other thriving towns to find opportunity amidst change. He points to the fact that one Ohio community, with a sizable population of Japanese families who work as managers in the Honda plant, started a Saturday school program taught by Japanese-speaking teachers to satisfy the cultural needs of the new residents who were used to six-day-a-week public schools, instead of five.

"The community that resists change dies," he says. "We must be experimental. We must accept the psychological (as well as the economic) shifts."

> *...St. Paris should think about developing the kind of strategic plan that a business would, projecting several years into the future, answering such questions as "where do we want to be in 10, 20, 50 years."*

Superior
Nebraska

"We have to get together to plan, to dream, and then to find a way to make that dream a reality."

—comment from a hospital administrator in Superior.

The people of Superior, Nebraska (population 2,400), have heard about the theories that the Great Plains should be turned back to the buffalo. But they're not paying much attention to what outsiders say about their community's chances for survival. They prefer to take the bull, or buffalo, by the horns and take control of their own destiny.

What they are doing is learning how to work together, getting more people involved in local leadership, setting priorities for new projects under the guidance, mainly, of a core of volunteers who want their small town to keep up with changing times.

Superior is located in south-central Nebraska, near the Kansas border. It's 60 miles from an interstate highway, and the nearest large town, with 23,000 people, is a 50-mile drive away.

Some see the location as a handicap. They blame their remoteness, in part, for economic setbacks—the closing of two manufacturing plants that were the area's leading employers—that hit the community in recent years.

> *Superior is stubbornly self-sufficient. The town has an active retail community and all the main street storefronts are filled.*

Others see their location as a plus. Superior is stubbornly self-sufficient. The town has an active retail community and all the main street storefronts are filled. A modern medical center serves a population base of 8,000 in Nebraska and Kansas. A well-kept golf course provides recreation for the area, and a large reservoir and recreation area, just over the Kansas border, brings people into Superior to shop.

There's a high level of local loyalty and pride, as evidenced by the presence of two banks and two savings and loans, as well as two up-to-date groceries.

In response to the staggering loss of manufacturing jobs, and capitalizing on the unique atmosphere of the community, the people of Superior have rallied around a new focus for community development. They've staked out a claim to the title "Victorian Capital of Nebraska," exploiting the presence in town of a number of lovely Victorian-style homes. The theme is reinforced with the "Lady Vestey Festival," named for a turn-of-the-century native who rose to a position of prominence and wealth as one of the first female executives in the meat-packing industry after she moved to Chicago. Later, she married into English nobility, but she never forgot her hometown of Superior.

A unique celebration honoring Lady Vestey is held annually in the Spring. Through its first seven years, the event has grown stronger and stronger. The entire community gets involved and the town's limited hotel space is booked nearly a year in advance. By January, all the rooms in a 40-mile radius will be reserved.

> *It is important for the town's leaders to learn to think strategically if Superior is going to prosper.*

The festival idea resulted from the community's efforts to write a strategic plan. It has been important for the town's leaders to learn to think strategically if Superior is to prosper, believes the hospital's administrator. "We have to get together to plan, to dream, and then to find a way to make that dream a reality."

The hospital itself is one of Nebraska's rural health care success stories. From its own strategic planning, the hospital has cautiously but successfully expanded, making Superior a regional center for CAT scans and other new health care technologies. With the addition of a new emergency room, the hospital can provide even better services for the area.

Like so many other towns on the Plains, however, this one was in an economic bind during the farm crisis of the mid-80s. Here, though, the trauma was made worse by other economic setbacks. First, a World War II-vintage cement plant was closed, and 150 well-paid workers were laid off. A year later, a large meat-packer in a nearby community also closed, putting another 150 out of work. At about the same time, J.C. Penney closed the Superior store, and the community lost its largest local retailer. More recently, a cheese plant, where 170 employees produced mozzarella for the nation's pizzas, closed its doors.

> *Many communities would simply throw in the towel after such a series of disasters. But that's not Superior's style.*

Many communities would simply throw in the towel after such a series of disasters. But that's not Superior's style. In fact, some leaders believe the cement plant's closing may have had some positive impacts. Several said wages at the plant, running $18 an hour plus general benefits, were "artificially high" for the area, creating a false sense of security for the local economy. Its closing served as a wake-up call that prepared the area for the other closings.

While the economic base hasn't changed drastically since Superior was founded in 1872, there's lots of interesting economic activity, much of it related in some way to global economic transformation.

AGREX, a subsidiary of Mitsubishi, operates a space-age elevator here, and it exports internationally about 25% of the grain it ships, mainly via unit trains to Mexico. As the northernmost point on what was then the Santa Fe Railroad, Superior can transport locally grown products quickly and efficiently into the Southwest, Mexico and the Gulf. The Farmers Co-op has more than tripled its business volume in recent years. It now ships grain from the area directly to Mexico and the West Coast. And the recently closed cheese plant is now re-opened, employing 30 people in the production of bacteria to be used as an environmentally friendly fertilizer.

The owner of a local graphics business, whose custom-designed T-shirts promote the Victorian homes tour, is learning how to expand his market. He uses the latest computer graphics software for his T-shirt designs and is now supplying a mail order house in Nevada. He knew he couldn't survive on hometown sales alone. "You have to have a product you can sell outside," he said.

Many residents agree that businesses and communities must change and adapt if they're going to survive.

"Our town is doing business differently today," says a local veterinarian. He is typical of area business owners who are trying hard to stay at the cutting edge of their specialty. His large-animal practice serves about 1,000 farmers, and he and his two partners saw their business increase 17% in one recent year. The entire operation is heavily computerized, and they've started a newsletter to keep clients up-to-date on innovative practices and treatments.

> *"Our town is doing business differently today...If you don't change the way you think, your business will decline."*

"If you don't change the way you think, your business will decline," he says.

The two banks have learned that lesson, as well. Both the Farmers State Bank and Security National bought branches in smaller towns in Nebraska and over the border in Kansas. The Farmers State Bank also expanded into residential loans throughout Nebraska and has loan representatives in several larger towns as far as 200 miles away.

> *"You can't compete with Wal-Mart. You've got to find a niche" that stores like Wal-Mart can't fill.*

The local newspaper publisher figured he'd have to lay off at least two employees when the cement plant went under and he lost a large commercial customer. "Then I read an article in The Wall Street Journal about single fellas staying on the job in the country, while women had to go to the city to find work." His entrepreneurial response is a newsletter called "Country Connections" which matches up men and women who are looking for partners and want to stay in or return to rural areas. Its national circulation of 1,700 has saved the two jobs that were threatened, and the town has received lots of publicity, generated by features about the newsletter on CBS and National Public Radio and in The New York Times.

He says his own business, and the others that are flourishing, have had to learn to change with the times. "You can't compete with Wal-Mart. You've got to find a niche" that stores such as Wal-Mart can't fill. "If you sing a tale of woe, after a while everyone will believe it."

The town's strategic planning effort, called START for the acronym of the state economic development program that fostered it, has had a lot to do with changing local attitudes and developing new leadership. A series of leadership seminars designed to get more people active in community affairs has paid off. Besides the Lady Vestey Festival, the strategic plan led to construction of a trolley for tours of Victorian homes, a new track and field at the school, renovation of the band shell and several city park improvements. A downtown hotel was remodeled, using $1 million in grant money, and turned into a combination community/senior center with 14 affordable apartments. A new library was built.

People in Superior have made the choice to live here because of what the community has to offer. One community leader points to a number of young people, originally from Superior, who have moved back to town to start their own businesses or work at the family business. "There really are quite a few young people coming in, and that's what the town really needs," she says.

A local stockbroker, who moved here a few years ago, chose Superior from among 200 towns where he could have relocated. He likes the "tremendous community spirit" and he believes people here are "willing to take a chance."

> *A local stockbroker, who moved here a few years ago, chose Superior from among 200 towns where he could have relocated.*

And then there's one of the town's physicians. She had grown up and raised a family here, then she decided to change careers. Nine years later she returned and started a family medical practice—filling a void that had existed since the early '80s when the town lost all its physicians. Now the clinic has a staff of three doctors and two physician's assistants.

Not everything's okay in Superior, though. People say day care needs more attention. The school has a good reputation, but some parents wish it could offer more in math, science and foreign language. There aren't enough things for kids to do, and not enough jobs to keep them after high school or bring them back from college. The need for more loyalty to local businesses is heard here, too. Some people still hope that one of those mythical clean, light industries will come to town, create 100 high-paying jobs, and stay forever.

> *"We're just a microcosm of what's going on in the larger economy."*

But there's still an undeniable enthusiasm that folks say just wasn't here a few years back.

From an economic standpoint, Superior is trying to learn how to keep up with the highly volatile, increasingly global economy that every town, large or small, must face. Looking up and down main street, one local banker talks about how the face of retail has changed and is still changing. He points to stores that have opened—and closed—in recent years, and to storefront renovations that often accompany a retail expansion.

"Retailers have to change or go out of business," he says. "It's the same in every part of our economy here." He pauses and then reflects: "We're just a microcosm of what's going on in the larger economy."

Watsonville
California

"It always comes down to a spirit of the people in the community."

—comment from a Watsonville real estate developer and school board member.

The year 1989 was a big one for Watsonville, California (population 37,000). That spring, the United States Supreme Court held that the city's tradition of electing all City Council members at-large violated the voting rights of Hispanic residents. Just three weeks before the first district elections were scheduled, the city was damaged extensively by a major earthquake. It destroyed much of the city's historic downtown and demolished or damaged 1500 residences.

The city had a disaster plan, but city government did not communicate with its residents in a language other than English (in a community that is more than 60% Hispanic). Disaster teams were poorly prepared, since they had no bilingual staff members or Spanish language materials. People whose homes were destroyed or severely damaged congregated in a public park, where they elected their own tent city mayor. The town might have been headed for a crisis larger than the earthquake.

> *Less than a decade later, the quake was treated as a blessing by many community leaders.*

Yet, less than a decade later, the quake is treated as a blessing by many of Watsonville's current leaders. Six new City Council members (out of a total of seven) were elected right after the quake. After the resignation of the long-time city manager, the City Council hired a new one and went about the task of reinventing city government, all the while dealing with the challenges created by the quake and its aftermath. "We developed a council that was able to work together," says one of three Hispanics now on the City Council. "Big windows opened up for a lot of people." He says the City Council changed the city's traditional closed-door attitude to an open-door one. Dialogue with citizens became a standard, with the help of new hiring policies that brought in multi-lingual employees... and more compromise to get things done. "That's what we thought governance should be."

Today, as it begins implementing priorities of its strategic plan, Watsonville has a new view of itself. And while the city faces major challenges, local leaders are, for the most part, upbeat.

Situated in the fertile Pajaro Valley along Monterey Bay, Watsonville is literally locked in by agricultural land that produces three fruit or vegetable crops annually... land that leases for as much as $5000 per acre annually and, if sold, could bring ten times that.

Strawberries, apples, fresh flowers, lettuce and bushberries are the five biggest products, but more than 60 crops are grown commercially in Santa Cruz County. Of the 12,000 county residents employed directly in agriculture, most live in Watsonville, which has been a farm-family and immigrant-oriented community since it was founded in the 1850s. Recently, most of those immigrants have family roots in Mexico. In other eras, they came from China, Italy, Portugal, Croatia, Japan and the Philippines.

The economy is changing rapidly here, as Watsonville feels the global economic pressures that are impacting many small towns and rural communities throughout the nation. In the 1960s, Watsonville's canneries produced nearly half of the nation's frozen vegetables. The city was known then as the "frozen food capital of the world." By the mid-1980s, compe-

> *The economy is changing rapidly, as the community feels global economic pressures.*

tition from south of the border had captured nearly one-third of the U.S. frozen vegetable market. In response, local producers tried to reduce labor costs drastically, but their pay-cut proposals resulted in an 18-month strike. The workers finally won back some of the pay-cuts that had been threatened, but more and more business still found its way to Mexico or overseas.

Now, local union officials fear the same thing may be happening to fresh strawberry production, which has taken up some of the slack left by the closing of the canneries. "We can't (any longer) compete in agriculture or food processing as a low-price commodity leader," says an international representative for the Teamsters. "The survivors have defined a market niche," such as pre-packaged salad mixes instead of head lettuce. Or they are developing new markets overseas for unique products, such as the sparkling cider produced by a local firm that's been in business for 150 years.

> *Economic and social changes are bringing major challenges, among them a battle over annexation.*

Economic and cultural changes are bringing major challenges, among them a battle with the county over the city's plans to annex 216 acres of farm land for housing and manufacturing. On the social end of the scale, few job opportunities and little hope for the future have been blamed for rising gang violence.

The community's many challenges show up in the statistics book:

■ Unemployment that hovers near 30% seasonally.

■ A violent crime rate, though improving recently, that was 47% above the national average at one point.

■ Badly overcrowded housing, at a rate four times the county average.

■ A poorly educated population, with barely half of adults completing a high school education and low achievement scores among today's students.

These challenges are accompanied by other contextual issues, including battles among developers and environmentalists over proposed developments near wetlands and criticism of city plans to allow more shopping center developments with jobs that are mainly low-wage and part-time. "There has to be a balance between growth and environment," according to the program manager for a teen program known as Pajaritos. "The economy hasn't grown to meet the demand of the population," he continues. "We need to find the balance."

For Watsonville's mayor, there is no question about priorities. "As mayor, I'm stressing jobs," he says. But the focus will be on small companies that add to economic diversification, he said, like a new manufacturing plant with its 29 employees. He is not just interested in entry-level jobs: "We want to diversify into other areas that pay higher than agriculture." His viewpoint is that young people shouldn't have to leave their hometown to find decent work. A Watsonville native himself, the mayor put it this way: "When your children have to leave to better themselves, you get kind of annoyed."

> *For Watsonville's mayor, the priority for the future is more and better jobs.*

Through its focus on youth, sustainable community development is central to Watsonville's strategic plan.

The focus on youth came straight out of community meetings held as part of a strategic planning process that led to Watsonville's designation as a rural Enterprise Community, and it was a theme that was repeated again and again. The process included daytime, luncheon, and evening meetings. Spanish translation encouraged the city's Hispanics to attend.

"Given the divisions, we did well at forging consensus," says a local leader who helped facilitate several of the meetings. "We voted with adhesive dots... it was a real participatory process."

> *A strong focus on youth came straight from a strategic planning process and multiple community meetings.*

Environmentally sustainable development is another frequent topic of conversation in Watsonville, where the Chamber of Commerce packet includes flyers on preservation of the Monterey Bay National Marine Sanctuary and the local talk includes a lot of "growth vs. no growth" verbiage. One focus of local controversy is a city ordinance that requires new housing developments to include a provision for 25% affordable housing. "We value the earth," said the middle school principal. "There are lots of environmentalists here." On the other hand, she conceded, "I'm willing to protect ag lands but I would support development if it provided more low-income housing."

To the union leader, the question "is not growth or no growth, but what kind of growth." He looks at what urban sprawl has done to other (formerly) rural communities, and says he doesn't want to see Watsonville in the future as just more paved-over farmland. "We don't think agriculture is a thing of the past in California."

Watsonville's primary goal is to reduce unemployment and poverty. It has set specific, measurable objectives for intended outcomes: reduce unemployment to 1.5 times the statewide average by 2005; reduce the poverty rate to 1.5 times the county average by 2010.

A new youth job initiative is central to both objectives. "The biggest challenge is jobs," says a representative of the Pajaro Valley Chamber of Commerce. "We need local training so local people can stay here and support themselves." He points out that the second major priority is housing.

> *Watsonville's primary goal is to reduce unemployment and poverty.*

Others agree. As one woman explains, "We need a partnership of jobs *and* housing," emphasizing the word, *and.*

She's also highly supportive of efforts to revitalize the downtown area, which still has some empty blocks that were bulldozed after the earthquake. Many of the revitalization efforts downtown are beginning to bear fruit. The old city plaza has recently been renovated, with a new border of palm trees and a restored central gazebo. A new, Spanish-style parking garage adorns one block. A recently completed downtown youth center anchors another. A new business incubator is complete, as is a nearby intermodal transportation center. A downtown department store has opened in space left by a long time retailer that closed its doors not too many months ago. Cabrillo College is expanding a Watsonville Branch which borders the central plaza.

Activity is contagious. "What you feel in Watsonville now is... *life!*" according to a resident who is a real estate developer and school board member. "There's a can-do, we've been through the worst" attitude, he says. "It's a real joy to see." He describes Watsonville as, ultimately, "pragmatic." In his words, "Decisions get made, then people row in the same direction."

Although there are still some disagreements about what all should be in Watsonville's vision of the future, there is also a strong sense of unanimity about overall direction.

City government, especially the City Council and City Manager, get good marks for openness and responsiveness. Old wounds, which took a long time to heal after the Supreme Court mandated district elections, are finally healing.

A former City Council member, who became the city's first woman mayor, points out how the city came together in the spring of 1995 when devastating floods made thousands of Watsonville's neighbors homeless in a small, poor community just across the Pajaro River in Monterey County. Another town might have said that, since the damage was in another county, it was someone else's responsibility. But Watsonville responded mightily, and temporary housing, plus other assistance, was arranged. The Santa Cruz County Farm Bureau pitched in with lots of help for workers displaced by rising waters.

> *There are still some disagreements, but there is also a strong sense of unanimity about overall direction.*

The religious community is also active, with initiatives in human rights, housing, and homelessness. St. Patrick's Catholic Church illustrates this point well. The historic St. Patrick's was so badly damaged by the quake that it eventually had to be torn down, brick by brick, and then painstakingly restored. Now it serves 6100 churchgoers each Saturday and Sunday, with 10 services, half in Spanish. "The big issue in the parish is how to bring Mexican immigrants into contact with the English speakers," says the parish priest. Progress is slow, he admitted, but he says the earthquake helped, especially when, during reconstruction of the sanctuary, services were scheduled in a gymnasium nearby and no one could find "their" family pew. "The quake was kind of a leveler," he said. The pun is obvious.

Salud Para La Gente is a nonprofit health clinic that serves 70,000 people, mostly farm workers, from a tri-county area. The clinic's director sees the emphasis on youth as highly appropriate, and he makes a personal commitment to act as mentor to two or three younger, emerging leaders at any one time. He also sees lots of future opportunities for partnerships: "Agencies that didn't network in the past will have to collaborate in the future."

> *"Agencies that didn't network in the past will have to collaborate in the future."*

Officially and unofficially, Watsonville's vision is both hopeful and realistic. But no one sidesteps the significant issues ahead. The statement of "strategic vision for change" that appears in Watsonville's strategic plan underscores the concern for youth: "Our strategic vision for change is centered around youth." The statement also calls for a "comprehensive, coordinated, grassroots approach to community revitalization."

In the vision statement itself, there are references to streets free from gangs and drugs, secure, year-round jobs, affordable housing for "everyone" (*everyone* is underlined), and neighborhood schools with plenty of parent involvement.

Goals for the next 10 years are articulated in a section that answers, point by point, the critical questions that evaluate progress:

"What will we do by when?"

"What will we change?"

"How will we measure the change?"

Those questions, and answers to them, are summarized under subheadings with titles such as "economic opportunity" and "human development." More importantly, perhaps, at the start of a decade of planned change, is what leaders themselves say about measures of success.

The new program coordinator for the Youth Job Training Program believes that once her program shows that young people can be trained for good jobs, "the whole community will see the benefit of the program" and it "can influence others to follow." A representative of the Chamber of Commerce wants to see "quantifiable changes" such as "the number of kids helped, the amount income has increased, the number of jobs available."

> *"This is a good opportunity for a lot of youth. Something to look forward to besides being in the streets."*

For the union leader, the future will include an "industrial policy" that differentiates between "good business" and "any business" or between "a good job" and "any job." The School Board member, who owns an insurance agency, believes a 10-year assessment of success will find "more Hispanic representatives in office."

A group of young adults, some dropouts themselves, are pleased with the opportunity to talk about the youth employment program and what it might mean to the community.

"This is a good opportunity for a lot of youth," says one youth. "Something to look forward to besides being in the streets."

Wausa
Nebraska

"This corner of the earth smiles on me."

—a quotation from Homer, seen in a store in downtown Wausa.

The main street of Wausa, Nebraska, at first glance, is typical of many small midwestern towns. There is an impression of attention paid to detail, of everyday life that is orderly and predictable and, above all, a feeling of solid, continuing history. The awareness of staying power is evident in the not-so-new but serviceable store fronts and the work clothes of the customers who shop there. This is a community that was founded in a determined fashion by Swedish immigrants about 100 years ago. It has survived because the attitudes of the founders have continued to the present. As one resident observed, "When our great-grandparents arrived here, they knew we'd be coming along some day. They built this town for their families and their descendants."

> *"I guess there's nothing really special about our town, unless you think it's unusual these days for people to care about keeping things in good order."*

Today, some 600 people live in Wausa. Although a high percentage of the community is in the 60-plus age group, the numbers of students in the school's classrooms is relatively stable and the population is holding steady. One church member noted, "During one recent month, the community saw four deaths and five births."

People here believe that their town is an excellent example of a well-kept, friendly midwestern community. "I guess there's nothing really special about our town, unless you think it's unusual these days for people to care about keeping things in good order," said one community leader.

Appearance is definitely seen as a strong point by community members and, although a few empty residences are in evidence, substandard or vacant housing does not seem to be a problem. The residential streets—mostly paved—are all well maintained. Homes show evidence of the owners' care and pride.

The people of Wausa are proud of the Community Hall (which can hold gatherings of 1,200), the school facilities and the nursing home, all physical evidence of the solidity and perseverance of the community. While community members might not discuss the appearance of their business district or the medical/dental clinic as symbols of the strength of the community, there can be no doubt that people do recognize the importance of these community assets to the future of their town. "We've always worked hard to keep health services in the town," said one community leader. "It makes all the difference in the number of people from other towns who come here for services and then stay to shop. We're very lucky that our professionals are committed to the community, too."

"Leadership here is seen as getting the right person to get the job done. There really isn't any one group that controls things," observed a lifetime resident. This pragmatic approach is typical of the town.

The formal leadership of the community is focused on the Village Board and several organizations such as the Community Club (renamed from the Commercial Club a few years ago in an effort to broaden membership beyond

> *"We've always worked hard to keep health services in town," said a community leader. "It makes all the difference in the number of people from other towns who come here for services and then stay to shop. We're very lucky that our professionals are committed to the community, too."*

business interests) and a Women's Club. In Wausa, perhaps because of its small size, leadership roles appear to be quite fluid and change easily. The regulars at the local cafe, elected officials, officers of clubs and those in charge of community projects are often all the same people. Leadership is diffused, but recognizable.

Leaders recognize that the community is best served by sharing opportunities for community service. Women have found their way into leadership positions and conscious efforts are made to include newcomers and younger community members in projects and tasks that serve as training ground for continued community service. While this type of mentoring behavior is described as "giving the young kids a turn at handling the jobs," it provides a smooth transition to new leadership for the community.

> *A younger leadership group, with an average age of less than 40, also indicates a positive trend among the downtown businesses in Wausa.*

Existence of a younger leadership group, with an average age of less than 40, also indicates a positive trend among the downtown businesses in Wausa. Family-owned firms with two active generations at work represent many of main street businesses in the community. But there are also several business owners who have adopted Wausa as their own and plan to stay.

These young managers also form the nucleus of a group working on economic development efforts. Organized as an Economic Development Corporation, they persisted in the successful effort to get a Community Development Block Grant to help a main street business expand. Currently, the group is using an innovative strategy to bring jobs to the town. They are searching for a small business to buy and relocate in Wausa. The search has not yet been productive, but support for the concept remains strong.

Equally as important as the need for job opportunities is the need for affordable housing for those who want to live and work in Wausa. The town is looking at building a few housing units for the elderly in order to free up homes for young families. Tax credits available for limited income housing might help finance such a project, but selling it to Wausa's older residents may be difficult. "Our people are pretty self-reliant and proud of living on their own," one community member said.

Located in the northeastern part of Nebraska, Wausa is 45 miles from Norfolk and 40 miles from Yankton, South Dakota. The trade area for Wausa exceeds what might be predicted for the town. Local businesses, which offers sales and services in an area described as "from river to river," explain their sizable sales territory by affirming that they sell service, not products. "There are some towns nearby where I've sold nearly every family a product," explained the owner of one family business.

Wausa's large trade area leads to a feeling that the town is a partner with other nearby communities. Recently city officials found themselves in a position of being statewide leaders for rural school interests during funding debates in the state legislature, something one Wausa resident called a "positive experience" for the town. "I think Wausa is generally respected as a community that gets along," he said.

> *"There are some towns nearby where I've sold nearly every family a product," explained the owner of one family business.*

Changes in the agricultural economy have had an impact on Wausa, but community leaders recognize that their community is not as severely affected as some towns. The reason, they say, is that few local farmers had been tempted to expand beyond their capabilities. Some mentioned that the soil in the area is too heavy to be improved by irrigation, so little or no debt was incurred to buy extensive irrigation systems. Others point to the frugal traditions of their Swedish heritage that have kept Wausa residents from overspending their good sense.

> *"Our people are really cautious about spending money they don't have, but at the same time they are willing to invest in their businesses when they have a chance to make the town better,"* said one member of the Economic Development Corporation.

"Our people are really cautious about spending money they don't have, but at the same time they are willing to invest in businesses when they have a chance to make the town better," said one member of the Economic Development Corporation. Noted another, "We've had to be really persistent in getting help from state agencies and outside programs, but it's been worth all the hassle and paperwork. Even a small program can make a difference in a town this size."

It may be a combination of such inherited traits that results in a vision of a future Wausa that preserves the present sense of small town security, cooperation, and common sense. While few if any residents want their community to be much changed in the future, there are groups within the community who discuss the hopes and fears, threats and opportunities represented by the future.

"I'd like to see a few more small businesses, maybe more jobs that aren't dependent on agriculture but, you know, I wouldn't trade the small town atmosphere for a shopping center," said one leader. "I think one of the things we do right in this town is to understand that to keep what we enjoy here, we have to keep up with modern changes and try to control what happens to our community."

> *"I think one of the things we do right in this town is to understand that to keep what we enjoy here we have to keep up with modern changes and try to control what happens to our community."*

Wray
Colorado

"We all want to make Wray an even better place."

—comment from a Prairie Commitment member.

How do community leaders shape a vision for the future and communicate that vision to others in the community? How do leaders build a consensus that supports a vision of the future and motivates community members to work together toward a shared goal? How do leaders persist in driving forward no matter how difficult or seemingly impossible the goal?

In Wray, Colorado, leaders have found answers to those questions.

Situated in the northeastern plains of Colorado, Wray is considered Centennial Country, a reference to the Michener novel that celebrated the hardy ranchers who settled there. It's true that the community of Wray is what most would call remote and isolated, but the achievements of this small western town would make any size community proud.

This town of 2,000 is nestled between the north fork of the Republican River and the white limestone bluffs near the Kansas and Nebraska borders. The commitment to farming and ranching is strong here. Yuma County is one of the largest corn growing counties in the nation, thanks to hard work and center-pivot irrigation.

> *"I look around and see a town that really wants to be here."*

The residents of Wray have always been proud of the quality of life they enjoy here. The town has a reputation for welcoming newcomers and supporting neighbors, as well as surviving hard times. "I look around and see a town that really wants to be here," explains the pastor of one of Wray's larger churches.

People here are proud of the churches and the Ministerial Association that collaborates on many social service and youth projects. They're proud of the Art Guild and the annual art show it sponsors with more than 300 entries from the area. A strong, diverse main street business community has helped the town remain strong over the years.

Visitors to Wray comment on the beautiful school facility on its 70-acre site. Education is a priority—as evidenced by the fact that Wray students are consistent winners in the annual statewide academic decathlon competition—and there are active connections between the school and the community.

For example, the Wray Task Force, formed of students, parents and teachers, has won the praise of the state of Colorado for its work in drug abuse prevention. The Task Force works to decrease teenage drinking in town and has developed many alternative activities for youngsters, as well as peer counseling and mentoring programs. According to one school administrator, "This community is remarkable for broad involvement in decision-making. These folks are really good problem solvers."

> *"This community is remarkable for broad involvement in decision-making. These folks are really good problem solvers."*

But "broad involvement in decision-making" doesn't just happen. It requires a conscious decision and a concerted effort to include as many people as possible in planning and working for projects that affect a large portion of the community. Leaders in Wray have put in long, hard hours to gain public input, understanding and support of the community's vision of the future—and it has paid off, big time.

One unique project best exemplifies how the principle of broad community involvement has been put to work in Wray.

For more than 20 years, there had been discussion of building an indoor center to house both recreation and rehabilitation activities. The combination of recreation and rehabilitation into one community facility is a sterling example of strategic thinking on the part of Wray's leadership. With a combined facility, both leisure and health needs could be met, and a considerable enhancement would be applied to the community's quality of life. Several age groups would be served by such a building.

> *The combination of recreation and rehabilitation into one community facility is a sterling example of strategic thinking on the part of Wray's leadership.*

Community leaders finally got tired of talking about the idea and decided to do something about it.

First, they surveyed the community to assess the need and level of support for a Wray Rehabilitation and Activities Center (WRAC). The majority of residents thought it was a great idea but were doubtful that it could be done. It seemed like an idea that might be too big for the town.

Encouraged by the support and determined to proceed, the nine members of the WRAC board began with the idea that about $300,000 was needed to remodel an old school building for use as the rehabilitation and recreation center. However, dreams have a way of growing and spreading out in Wray, and the board members soon found themselves developing a brand new building project that would require nearly $2 million to complete.

Fund-raising is a task that often presents almost insurmountable obstacles for small communities. The WRAC board members, however, took on the job of raising money with great energy and creativity. They organized almost every fund-raising event possible, from rubber duck races on the river to "Mayor for a Day" certificates that required a mere $20 contribution.

While these types of community events weren't the primary source of funding, they did help keep the populace informed and aware of the project and thus served an educational and marketing purpose.

The enthusiasm also caught the eye of those in a position to make major contributions to the project. Through a combination of private donations, gifts from trusts and foundations, state funds, and contributions from corporations, the goal of $1.8 million was reached and the WRAC has become a reality.

Since its opening, the popularity of the center has surpassed even the most enthusiastic expectations. Citizens of all ages enjoy the year-round recreation programs. Recuperative therapy draws people from throughout northeastern Colorado, and physical recovery from surgery or accident is quicker and more complete. While much of the work at the center is done by volunteers, it also provides new employment opportunities, especially for the community's young people. Much of the positive activity in Wray is now centered at the WRAC.

> *Since its opening, the popularity of the center has surpassed even the most enthusiastic expectations. Citizens of all ages enjoy the year-round recreation programs.*

Interestingly, the age group once most skeptical about the establishment of such a facility in Wray has quietly become its biggest fan. Senior citizens have discovered how enjoyable it is to improve both the physical and social aspects of their lives through regular use of WRAC programs.

Completion of the WRAC marked a major milestone in the history of Wray. It had taken more than five years of weekly 6 a.m. meetings—as well as countless hours along the way—for the WRAC board to hold the project together and pull it off.

But community leaders weren't satisfied to rest on their laurels. They had already embarked on another major undertaking.

> *Community leaders weren't satisfied to rest on their laurels. They had already embarked on another major undertaking.*

Improved and expanded facilities to provide medical care for the people of Wray, as well as a rural area including parts of northeastern Colorado and southwestern Nebraska, had been identified as a top priority through town hall meetings and community surveys. Again, the project seemed almost too big to tackle. And, once more, the folks of Wray were ready to accept the challenge.

Construction of a state-of-the-art hospital would require a $6.5 million bond issue. But under a Colorado law limiting the amount of bonded indebtedness allowed for special districts, the Wray hospital district could only issue bonds for less than half that amount. Undeterred, community leaders convinced the state legislature to change the law.

Wray citizens gave resounding approval to the bond issue and the ultra-modern Wray Community District Hospital became the first rural hospital built in Colorado in 29 years.

The regional facility offers comprehensive in-patient and out-patient care, including scheduled and emergency surgery, and is staffed by three family practice physicians, a general surgeon, a physician's assistant, a nurse practitioner, and two family practice residents. Four of the medical staff were either born or raised in Wray and chose to return home to practice.

Because of its ability to get things done, this small rural community has been widely hailed in development circles. The community's far-sightedness and perseverance in developing the WRAC and the hospital was cited by judges when Wray was named an All-America City.

But more important than winning awards are the lessons learned along the way. Turning dreams into reality has taught community leaders just how much can be accomplished when you set goals and work hard to achieve them. They've also come to realize that making their community a better place is an ongoing process. "No matter how well we may have done in the past, the challenge of change never goes away," says one of those involved.

Meeting that challenge is the mission of Prairie Commitment, an open-membership group that welcomes anyone with an interest in area betterment and a willingness to accept challenges.

> *"No matter how well we may have done in the past, the challenge of change never goes away."*

The group has adopted a broader mission and a lower profile than was necessary to accomplish the WRAC and hospital projects. Regular weekly meetings are gone, but the Prairie Commitment group stands ready to dive in whenever the need arises. Their role now, according to one member, is to support all aspects of community development and to make sure people in the community are well informed about what's going on.

The pace has slowed down in Wray. Maybe it's time to take a hard look at where the town is and where it's going, one Prairie Commitment member says. "It's amazing to look back at where we were just a few years ago and compare it to where we are today—and it's almost scary to try to envision where we'll be in five or ten years. But one thing's for sure. We're not afraid to take that look."

> *"Picture it…but better yet, change visions to creations, change imagination to fact…"*

Goal-setting is a skill that's based on the ability to project the preferred future. Project planning takes the skill to see the individual tasks necessary to reach the goal. Both are learnable.

But that vision of the future and the inspiration it takes to persevere are qualities of leadership that represent real community treasures.

As one community leader from Wray has written, "Picture it…but better yet, change visions to creations, change imagination to fact…"

The people of Wray, Colorado, are doing just that.

About the Heartland Center

The Heartland Center for Leadership Development is an independent, nonprofit organization developing local leadership that responds to the challenges of the future. A major focus of the Heartland Center's activities is developing and sharing practical resources for rural community survival. Heartland Center programs, while designed with small towns in mind, have also been useful to professionals working in the urban and suburban environments.

The Heartland Center was organized in 1985 by a group of Great Plains leaders as an outgrowth of Visions from the Heartland, a grassroots futures project. Today, the Center is known throughout North America and internationally for its field research on Clues to Rural Community Survival and its hands-on programs in community leadership development.

Heartland Center programs and publications stress the critical role played by local leadership as communities and organizations face the challenges associated with changing times. Programs of the Center emphasize that local capcity is critical...and renewing local leadership essential...as towns, cities and states work to remain competitive today and in the future.

Heartland Center for Leadership Development
941 'O' Street, Suite 920, Lincoln, NE 68508
Phone: 402-474-7667 or 800-927-1115   Fax: 402-474-7672
www.4w.com/heartland/

Milan Wall

Milan Wall, co-director of the Hearland Center for Leadership Development, is a management and communications expert with more than 25 years experience in dealing with the critical issues facing American society and culture.

Mr. Wall has been a newspaper reporter and editorial columnist, a university lecturer and a speaker at regional and national conferences on such topics as educational leadership, economic development, and uses of technology in education. Before he helped found the Heartland Center, he was Executive Vice President of the University of Mid-America, a multi-state consortium that was recognized internationally for its imaginative approaches to adult education.

With Dr. Vicki Luther, he is co-author of a number of publications on leadership and community development, including The Entrepreneurial Community: A Strategic Leadership Approach to Community Survival, Clues to Rural Community Survival, and Schools as Entrepreneurs: Helping Small Towns Survive. Previously, he served as editor of the Nebraska School Leader, which won three national awards for excellence among state publications on education during his tenure.

In 1993, Mr. Wall was honored with the Award of Excellence, the distinguished alumni recognition of the University of Nebraska-Lincoln Teachers College.

Vicki Luther

Vicki Luther, co-director of the Heartland Center for Leadership Development, has over 20 years experience in a variety of programs designed to increase citizen participation in government and to improve the skills of decision-makers in both the public and private sectors. Her experience applying strategic planning to rural issues includes working at the local level in small towns as well as with policy makers throughout the Midwest.

As co-director and a founder of the Heartland Center for Leadership Development with Milan Wall, she has developed training programs for community leaders and has participated in research projects on economic development and healthy communities. The author of several articles on futuring, community planning and leadership training, she is also the co-author of several publications on rural community development. Luther received the 1992 National Community Development Society Achievement Award for her work in the area of community development.

A cum laude graduate of Marywood College, she received a masters degree in culture change from Central Washington University and an Ph.D. in Educational Leadership from Gonzaga University in Spokane. In 1998, she completed the Masters Class for Leadership Educators at the Kennedy School of Government, Harvard University.